BORDERS OF LAKELAND

Caldbeck Church and Bridge (H.William Reading)

Thirty-one Walks
on the

Borders of Lakeland

described by

Robert Gambles

Assisted by
Hanna Gambles and Beryl Richardson

Illustrations by
Margaret Woods and H.William Reading

CICERONE PRESS
Milnthorpe, Cumbria

ISBN 1 85284 162 1
A catalogue record for this book is available from the British Library.

ACKNOWLEDGEMENTS

The authors wish to express their appreciation to Margaret Woods and to H.William Reading who gave so generously of their time and skills to produce most of the sketches which illustrate this guide.

The bird illustrations are from Thomas Bewick's *History of British Birds* (1804) and the animal illustrations are from his *General History of Quadrupeds* (1807).

The sources of all other illustrations are acknowledged below the accompanying captions.

By the same author
Man in Lakeland
Place Names of the Lake District
Out of the Forest: The Natural World and the Places-names of Cumbria
The Spa Resorts and Mineral Springs of Cumbria

and with Beryl Richardson
Exploring the Lakeland Fringe

Front Cover: Ennerdale

CONTENTS

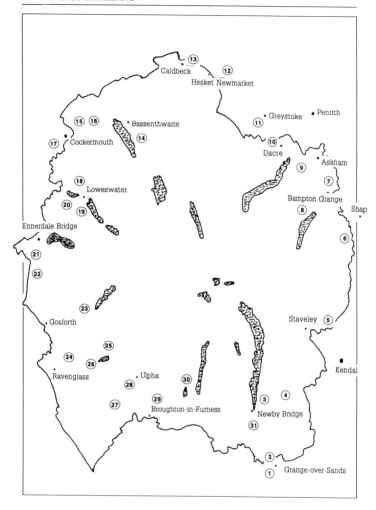

LOCATION OF WALKS

6

List of Walks

ADVICE TO READERS

Readers are advised that whilst every effort is taken by the authors to ensure the accuracy of this guidebook, changes can occur which may affect the contents. New fences and stiles appear, waymarking alters, there may be new buildings or eradication of old buildings. It is advisable to check locally on transport, accommodation, shops etc. but even rights of way can be altered, paths can be eradicated by landslip, forest clearances or changes of ownership. The publisher would welcome notes of any such changes.

PREFACE

In their book *Exploring the Lakeland Fringe* the authors described the many delights to be found in walking through the unfrequented countryside on the boundary of the Lake District National Park. In these quiet marches, away from the often overcrowded central areas, there are scenes of outstanding natural beauty which if they were not always in the shadow of so much overwhelming mountain splendour would be more readily appreciated. Here, too, there is much of interest for the historian and the archaeologist while the botanist and wildlife enthusiast will find riches almost lacking in those places subject to popular tourist pressure.

A great deal had to be omitted from the 150 miles of walks described in *Exploring the Lakeland Fringe* and the thirty-one walks included here attempt to remedy this, embracing such fascinating outposts of the National Park as Nannycatch Gate, The Howk, Monk's Bridge and the ancient stone circle at Swinside. There are many splendid and surprising views of the high fells seen from unfamiliar angles, often combined with breathtaking panoramas of the western sea as on Hampsfell or from the ancient "City of Barnscar". On these routes are historic castles such as Dacre and Muncaster, country mansions such as Isel Hall and Mirehouse and picturesque churches such as Cartmel Priory and Saint Bega's on the shore of Lake Bassenthwaite.

All the walks follow public rights of way or permissive footpaths and apart from a few eccentric stiles should present no great difficulty to walkers of all ages.

NOTE ON MAPS

The maps which accompany the text for each walk are intended as route guides only. Even in the sometimes remote and unfrequented countryside covered by many of these walks they should, in conjunction with the directions given, provide clear guidance, but there can be no substitute for the Ordnance Survey Pathfinder and Outdoor Leisure Maps and it is recommended that these should be used for fuller detail of the terrain and topography. The four Lake District Outdoor Leisure Maps cover only sections of the area covered by these thirty-one walks on the borders of Lakeland and a number of the Pathfinder Maps are also required. Their references are given by each walk.

The principal symbols used in the maps are as follows:

A	=	the point at which each walk begins and ends
→	=	the direction of the route as described in the text
⟿	=	optional or alternative routes
xxxx	=	the boundary of the Lake District National Park
S.P.	=	signpost
F.B.	=	footbridge
☼	=	viewpoint
T	=	Public Telephone
P	=	Official Parking Areas (These are sparsely provided and it is often necessary to find parking space wherever convenient; this is not usually difficult except during busy week-ends. Where appropriate, suggestions are given in the text at the start of each walk.)

The compass rose on each map is a representation of the plan of the Stone Circle at Swinside.

Local Authorities and the National Park Service have recently undertaken a great deal of work in erecting and renovating signposts, stiles and gates, and this has made it easier to keep to the right of way and to avoid trespass. There may occasionally be slight changes in the exact direction of a footpath as the result of agreements between the farmer and the appropriate authority; where this does occur the new direction is usually indicated on the spot and should always be followed.

List of Walks and associated Ordnance Survey Maps

1	Humphrey Head	Pathfinder SD 37/47
2	Hampsfell and Cartmel Priory	Pathfinder SD 37/47 & 48/58
3	Cartmel Fell and Sow How Tarn	Pathfinder SD 48/58
4	Whitbarrow	Pathfinder SD 48/58
5	Potter Fell	Outdoor Leisure - Lakes SE
6	Wet Sleddale	Outdoor Leisure - Lakes NE
7	Knipe Scar	Outdoor Leisure - Lakes NE
8	Bampton Common and Haweswater	Outdoor Leisure - Lakes NE
9	Moor Divock and Heughscar Hill	Outdoor Leisure - Lakes NE
10	Dacre and Hutton John	Outdoor Leisure - Lakes NE
11	Greystoke	Pathfinder NY 43/53 & O.L. NE
12	Castle How and Newlands Mill	Pathfinder NY 23/33
13	Watersmeet and the Howk	Pathfinder NY 23/33
14	Bassenthwaite and Dodd Wood	Outdoor Leisure - Lakes NW
15	Isel, Blindcrake and Sunderland	Pathfinder NY 03/13
16	Isel and the River Derwent	Pathfinder NY 03/13
17	Cockermouth and the River Cocker	Outdoor Leisure - Lakes NW
18	Low Fell	Outdoor Leisure - Lakes NW
19.	Crummock Water Scale Force and Mosedale	Outdoor Leisure - Lakes NW
20.	Loweswater	Outdoor Leisure - Lakes NW
21.	Flat Fell and Nannycatch Gate	Outdoor Leisure - Lakes NW
22.	Tongue Moor and the River Calder	Outdoor Leisure - Lakes SW
23.	Nether Wasdale	Outdoor Leisure - Lakes SW
24.	Muncaster Fell	Outdoor Leisure - Lakes SW
25.	Stanley Ghyll	Outdoor Leisure - Lakes SW
26.	Devoke Water and Barnscar	Outdoor Leisure - Lakes SW
27.	Swinside Stone Circle	Pathfinder SD 08/18
28.	Ulpha Park and Frith Hall	Outdoor Leisure - Lakes SW
29.	The Lickle valley & Appletreew'th Beck	Outdoor Leisure - Lakes SW
30.	Beacon Tarn and Beacon Fell	Pathfinder SD 28/38 & O.L. SW
31.	Bigland Tarn and Bigland Barrow	Pathfinder SD 28/38

THE COUNTRY CODE

Enjoy the countryside and respect its life and work
Guard against all risk of fire
Fasten all gates
Keep dogs under close control
Keep to public paths across farmland
Use gates and stiles to cross fences, hedges and walls
Leave livestock, crops and machinery alone
Take litter home
Help to keep all water clean
Protect wildlife, plants and trees
Take special care on country roads
Make no unnecessary noise.

Black-headed gull (Peter Gambles)

Badger (Sarah Mattocks)

Walk 1:
Humphrey Head

Base Point:	Humphrey Head - 2m/3.25km south-west of Grange-over-Sands
Map:	Pathfinder SD 37/47
Grid Reference:	SD 393733
Distance:	2m/3.25km

The starting point for this walk is by the entrance to the Field Centre along the narrow lane which runs on the west side of Humphrey Head. There is space to park three or four cars here; otherwise it is necessary to go ¹/₂ mile further along the lane to park on the shore well above the tide-line.

Humphrey Head is a limestone promontory extending into the sands and the tidal waters of Morecambe Bay, with steep and dangerous cliffs on the west side and a gentler slope on the east. The cliffs, woodlands and grassy top and the extensive mudflats which surround the headland are well known for the variety of flora and birdlife to be seen there. Most of the headland is a Nature Reserve and Site of Special Scientific Interest, now known as The Joy Ketchen Reserve. The walk goes along the sheep-grazed turf for the whole length of the headland rising to the Ordnance Survey Column at the 150 feet summit and then gently down to the rocky tip, returning along the east side and passing through the woods with their surprisingly robust and numerous oak trees. It is advisable to keep well clear of the cliff edge and, if one ventures on to the shore, to beware of deep channels and fast in-coming tides.

The walk begins at a kissing gate at the beginning of the entrance drive to the Field Centre where a notice-

Thrift (Peter Gambles)

13

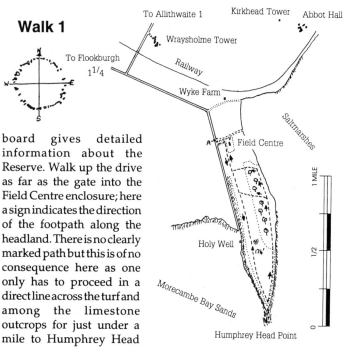

Walk 1

To Allithwaite 1

Kirkhead Tower

Abbot Hall

Wraysholme Tower

To Flookburgh
1¹/₄

Railway

Wyke Farm

Saltmarshes

A — Field Centre

1 MILE

Holy Well

¹/₂

Morecambe Bay Sands

0

Humphrey Head Point

board gives detailed information about the Reserve. Walk up the drive as far as the gate into the Field Centre enclosure; here a sign indicates the direction of the footpath along the headland. There is no clearly marked path but this is of no consequence here as one only has to proceed in a direct line across the turf and among the limestone outcrops for just under a mile to Humphrey Head Point, with the vast seascape unfolding if the day is clear.

At the fence and stile, near the point, the path returns along the east side keeping on the inland side of the fence, but before starting along this path an exploration over the rocks at the very point of the headland will, at the appropriate season, reveal a wealth of colourful flowers and plants and interesting pools left behind by the outgoing tide. Rejoin the path over the stile. A line of sturdy, wind-blasted trees adorns the rocky shore and many waders and other wildfowl feed on the mudflats beyond. Continue to a stile which gives access to the woodland and follow the well-trodden path for about ¹/₂ mile to a point where it divides. Either fork may be chosen: the left path goes up to a stile in the boundary wall to rejoin the outward path; the right-hand path continues to the end of the wood and goes to another stile a short distance further along the wall. From either

14

Humphrey Head (Margaret Woods)

route go straight ahead from the wall to return to the main path a few minutes away from the Field Centre.

Humphrey Head was once the property of the Canons of Cartmel Priory and achieved fame by virtue of its "Holy Well", a saline spring much frequented by all sorts and conditions of men for many hundreds of years and, even today, there are those who seek it out for its alleged medical and spiritual benefits. It was visited in the seventeenth century by Sarah Fell of Swarthmoor Hall and in the eighteenth century by Thomas Browne of Townend, Troutbeck, and until the early twentieth century its waters were consumed in large quantities by the lead miners of Alston who believed this to be the cure for the poison absorbed by their bodies in the course of their work. Others placed their faith in the waters for the treatment of various skin diseases, ague, worms and jaundice. In 1867 a chemical analysis pronounced the waters at Humphrey Head to be comparable to those of such famous Spa resorts as Cheltenham, Baden-Baden and Wiesbaden, and plans were soon afoot to build a Pump Room, Spa Hotel and Assembly Rooms to rival these prestigious centres of fashionable society. Fortunately this project did not come to fruition but the spring still flows at the foot of the cliffs at its steady rate of one gallon per minute.

Walk 2:

Hampsfell and Cartmel Priory

Base Point:	Off the B5271 near Lindale
Map:	Pathfinder SD 37/47 & 48/58
Grid Reference:	SD 213808
Distance:	7m/11.25km

Hampsfell is a limestone ridge above Grange-over-Sands with magnificent views over the Kent Estuary and Morecambe Bay. On a clear day this is a splendid viewpoint for an exhilarating vista of the Lakeland fells, from Black Combe in the west to the Howgills and Ingleborough in the east: more than fifty peaks in all. The walk to the summit at just over 700 feet is easy and on the plateau itself are grassy paths in all directions. Here, too, is a remarkable limestone pavement with deep fissures in which a variety of ferns and other plants find a congenial habitat. An unusual feature of Hampsfell summit is the Hospice, an interesting if less than elegant building, created by an enterprising Cartmel priest in the early nineteenth century for "the shelter and entertainment of travellers over the fell". It still admirably serves this purpose, with seats, a fireplace and four panels of homespun verse inside, and outside is a precipitous flight of steps to the

roof and a useful viewfinder. An inscription carved over the lintel of the east-facing door invites the visitor (in Greek) to "Hail the Dawn".

Hampsfell is the southernmost point of the Lake District National Park; the boundary passes across the fell just below the summit.

The walk starts on a minor road off the B5271 near Lindale where there is often parking space for a few cars. A signpost on this road points along a lane to Hampsfield and indicates that there is "No Through Road". Walk along

Cistercian monk (Sylvia Rigby)

Walk 2

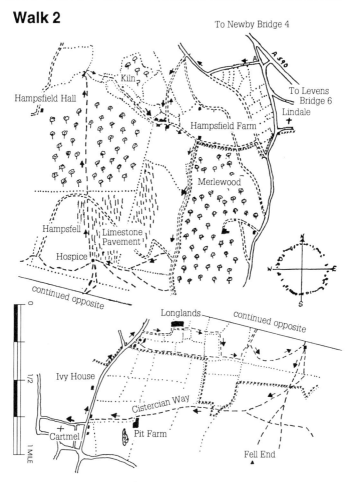

To Newby Bridge 4

Kiln

Hampsfield Hall

To Levens
Bridge 6

Lindale

Hampsfield Farm

Merlewood

Hampsfell

Limestone
Pavement

Hospice

continued opposite

Longlands

continued opposite

Ivy House

Cistercian Way

Cartmel

Pit Farm

Fell End

this lane for less than ¹/₂ mile and bear left by a house called "Redriggs" with a post box in the wall. In a short distance turn right almost opposite a large barn to join a path between walls which soon reaches a gate bearing instructions to "Follow the walls and markers". Obey this and you will be safely guided through woods and eventually to a gate into Merlewood: do not go through this gate but follow the wall round to the right. Turn left at the corner of the wall with the open fell on the right. Keep to the wall until a footpath sign indicates the way to Hampsfell.

The network of paths and sheep trods here may seem confusing but by pursuing a consistent upward course bearing left and aiming for the corner where the walls meet you will come to a stile about 100 metres below this point. Over the stile turn sharp right and the summit and the Hospice will soon come into view.

The next stage of the walk may be regarded as an optional extra or, indeed, as a short round walk in its own right. Its main objective is to visit the charming and unspoilt village of Cartmel and, especially, its ancient and imposing Priory Church. The descent from Hampsfell is an easy stroll; the return takes longer but is no great challenge.

Take the path leading from the south side of the Hospice towards the wall. There is a choice of two stiles here, only a few yards apart: either will lead to a clear grassy track, part of the track now known as the Cistercian Way. Turn right at the junction with another wide track and follow the footpath signs down from the fell and into the valley fields with the village and church straight ahead. The footpath sign by Pit Farm bears a small figure of a Cistercian monk pointing the way to his Priory across the last field.

Turn left where the path emerges on to the road and, in a few metres, take the first road on the right. This leads directly to the Priory and the centre of the village, a delightful square with the impressive Gatehouse of the Priory, several excellent hostelries, a distinguished bookshop, a number of charming houses, and, just beyond, the country's most captivating racecourse.

The Augustinian Priory of Cartmel was founded in 1189 by William Marshall, Earl of Pembroke, and was built, in all probability, on the site of an older church. It was also built on the only spot in the vicinity which, at that time, would bear the weight of such a massive structure, an egg-shaped crag almost surrounded by the waters of Lake Cartmel. This was a post-glacial lake which was not drained until the great expansion of agriculture about 200 years ago and so must have given the Priory a distinctly romantic setting throughout its life as a monastic foundation. After the Dissolution in 1537 the Priory Church was saved from destruction and survived as the Parish Church of Cartmel. Today its unique tower, set

*Cartmel Priory
(Cartmel Priory)*

*diagonally across the transept lantern, looks out over the green meadows
and damp marshes where once the waters of the lake glistened in the sun.
This "Cathedral of the Lakes" still flourishes not only as a place of worship
but as the centre for festivals of fine music. The excellent guidebook on sale
in the Church outlines the main points of interest - and there are many -
and has some stunning illustrations. A fuller history by J.C.Dickinson,*
The Priory of Cartmel, *is published by Cicerone Press.*

For the return to Hampsfell it is possible to follow the Cistercian
Way used on the descent or to choose an alternative route via
Longlands. For this, walk for about ½ mile along the road past Ivy
House and turn into the driveway to Longlands. This bridleway
goes up to the house itself where it turns right, past the "Coach
House", and continues to a gap stile in a small boundary wall.
Beyond this proceed straight ahead to a field gate and on past an
impressive beech tree to a gate at the junction of the walls. (Ahead
on the fellside is a substantial stone tower built as a summer house
in more leisurely days.)

Through this gate keep close to the hedge on the right and in a
very short distance turn left to join a deeply rutted track coming in
from the farm below. Follow this up to a gateway giving access to
the open fellside. The track now swings sharply to the left but the
path to the summit goes to the right. No clearly defined path is
visible although there are numerous sheep trods. Climb steadily
towards the wall and just before reaching it bear to the left and
continue on an upward course towards the limestone outcrops
above. The first limestone pavement will soon be reached and from

19

there the Hospice stands only a short distance away.

The last leg of the walk begins on the north side of the Hospice, the side where the steps are. Follow a straight line away from the Hospice along a path below the limestone pavement and aim for a stile in the wall at the edge of the wood. From here a good, airy path goes down to a gate into a field. (A notable feature on this path is a large limestone boulder with a variety of plants growing in its fissures - a miniature natural rock-garden.)

Turn sharp right through the gate and in a few metres look for a gated stile high in the wall. Over this stile keep straight ahead with a plantation on the right and into a narrow field with an old lime-kiln under the trees. The path goes to the right of the kiln and along a walled lane directly to the farm at High Hampsfield. Turn left here to rejoin the lane at the post box by Redriggs; turn left again to return to the start of the walk.

Walk 3:
Cartmel Fell and Sow How Tarn

Base Point:	St Anthony's Church, Cartmel Fell
Map:	Pathfinder SD 48/58
Grid Reference:	SD 416881
Distance:	2¾m/3.66km

Cartmel Fell is a pleasant mixture of woodland and upland farmsteads overlooking the Winster Valley, a peaceful, pastoral scene largely undisturbed by Lakeland's tourist visitors but echoing in spring to the bleat of newborn lambs and in winter to the cries of the largest flocks of greylag geese in England.

Ravensbarrow, the highest point on the fell, looks down on land which has belonged in turn to the early Scandinavian settlers, to Stephen of Boulogne (later King of England), to the Augustinian Priors, to the Duchy of Lancaster and to the yeoman farmers who built their manor houses and halls along the valley: Hodge Hill, Thorphinsty, Cowmire, Witherslack and Burblethwaite. The 200 or 300 folk who lived in the parish made a living from sheep-farming, charcoal-burning, basket-weaving, leather-

Walk 3

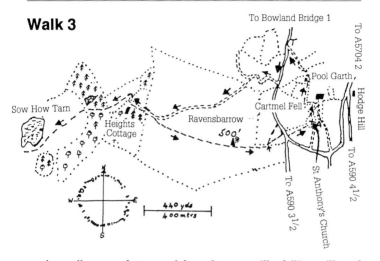

To Bowland Bridge 1

To A5704 2

To A590 4½

Hodge Hill

Pool Garth

Cartmel Fell

Ravensbarrow

500'

St Anthony's Church

To A590 4½

To A590 3½

Sow How Tarn

Heights Cottage

440 yds
400 mtrs

work, woollen manufacture and from the corn mills, fulling mills and bobbin mills.

Much of this has now vanished but, hidden among the trees, there still remains Cartmel Fell's beautiful little church, one of the gems of Lakeland. Built in 1504 and dedicated to St Anthony, the patron saint of charcoal burners and basket weavers, the church escaped the ravages of zealous Puritans and well-meaning Victorians and is still very much as it was 400 years ago. Its simple unadorned stonework, its oak-beamed roof, its fine east window, (a splendid example of English medieval glass,) and its unusual seventeenth-century three decker pulpit, give immediate pleasure to the eye, but there are other pleasures here too. A simple guidebook, on sale in the church, makes one's visit full of interest and what better place to rest a while? For this is a place of beauty and peace, once described as "one of the most magical little places in the whole of Cumbria".

The walk begins at the east end of the church where a gate gives access to a lane. Follow this for a short distance and where it turns sharply to the right keep to the left and cross over a small beck behind a house. Shortly after this turn right to cross a field to a gate near a house known as Pool Garth. Just beyond this gate, on the left, a field gate leads into a lane which is the driveway to the house. Follow this to the roadside and turn left up the hill. Soon after

St Anthony's Church, Cartmel Fell (William Reading)

negotiating the steep bends a field gate on the right marks the beginning of a wide farm track which winds its way uphill straight ahead.

Continue along this track until it approaches close to a wall and then swings away to the right. At this point go through a gate on the left to join a broad, grassy bridleway across the slopes of Ravensbarrow. As the path descends towards a wall it meets another at a T-junction.

Turn right here and aim for a white gate by a conifer plantation fringed by a number of rhododendron bushes. Beyond this is a barn-like building known as "Heights Cottage". Turn right here and almost immediately swing to the left along a track which soon enters a wood.

Keep to the main path through the wood and then cross a field to reach Sow How Tarn, a reservoir but none the less idyllic for that, a pleasant spot to pause before the return journey. Return by the same route, past Heights Cottage and to the T-junction on Ravensbarrow. From here take the path which leads up to the summit of the fell marked by a prominent and substantial cairn which commands a splendid view over the Winster Valley.

From the summit a path goes westward, towards the church,

St Anthony's Church, seventeenth-century pulpit (William Reading)

down to the road where a signpost points the way down a narrow pathway to "St Anthony's Church". A stone stile gives access to the churchyard just by the west tower.

Walk 4:
Whitbarrow

Base Point:	Lyth Valley Hotel
Map:	Pathfinder SD 48/58
Grid Reference:	SD 453896
Distance:	4¹/₂m/7.3km

Whitbarrow is a massive limestone ridge with an impressive escarpment on the western side. It was once a headland projecting into the sea but now overlooks the marshes of the Kent Estuary and the flat pastures of the Lyth Valley drained of its tidal waters only 150 years ago. In common with most of the Carboniferous limestone areas of Southern Lakeland Whitbarrow is rich in its flora and fauna and has long been designated as a Nature

Walk 4

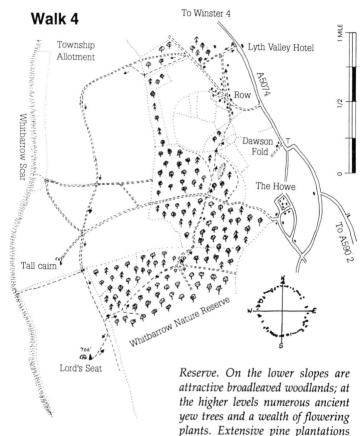

Reserve. On the lower slopes are
attractive broadleaved woodlands; at
the higher levels numerous ancient
yew trees and a wealth of flowering
plants. Extensive pine plantations
clothe the eastern side almost as far as the screes and pavements of the
summit ridge where the fissures in the rock provide a safe habitat for a
number of ferns and mosses, some of them as rare as the plants which grow
on the steep cliffs out of reach of both humans and sheep. The tall summit
cairn stands at a little over 700 feet above sea level; there can be few other
places which offer such a rewarding view from such a modest height. To the
west and north is a wide panorama of the Lakeland fells; to the east the
Whinfells, the Howgills and the long spine of the Pennines; to the south the

24

Morecambe Bay from Whitbarrow Scar (William Reading)

Lancashire coastline, the Irish sea and the vast sandscape of Morecambe Bay.

There is an almost infinite variety of walks to be enjoyed on Whitbarrow: this is just one of them.

The walk begins at the lay-by opposite the Lyth Valley Hotel. A signpost in the hedgerow points to a narrow footpath leading between hedges and walls, colourful with many plants and flowers, and punctuated with stray crab-apple and damson trees. In about 150 metres take the right-hand fork at a junction of paths and soon join a wide track with a wood on the right. Follow this for about 400 metres.

At a T-junction turn right along a straight drive through woodland and in less than 100 metres go through a gate on the left into a field pleasantly enhanced by a number of mature trees, probably the scattered remnants of a wood. The official right of way leads along the wall on the left to a stile at the far end but this path is now almost invisible and it is certainly easier to follow the broad track across to a gateway leading on to the open fell. Continue along the track for a good ¹/₂ mile until it swings round to the left.

There is now a veritable network of paths and sheep trods to cause confusion but keep to the main track with the plantation straight ahead and, in due course, a tall cairn will appear over to the right. When the boundary wall of the wood comes into view aim directly for a gate and stile a short distance below the cairn.

Over the stile the path proceeds straight ahead through a small area of birch trees and then along a limestone escarpment before turning to the right over the scree up to Lord's Seat, the summit of Whitbarrow Scar, with its grandstand view over land and sea

To continue the walk descend from the summit by the same route down to the limestone escarpment. Follow the path to the left as far as a stile in the wall. Enter the woodland and walk along a good path among many different types of trees for about $1/2$ mile to an important junction of paths in the centre of a group of mature oak trees. Here care should be taken to follow the correct route, otherwise it is easy to go astray among the numerous tracks in these woods: turn sharply to the left, and follow the path to a small gate in a wall.

Through the gate continue past a plantation of spruce to another junction with a clear track. Cross this and look for a waymark arrow pointing along a narrow path into the woods. In about 100 metres this path divides and here take the right fork which leads to a gap stile in the wall at the edge of the woodland.

There is no clear path beyond this but the route goes diagonally to the right through an old damson orchard and then across a field, in the same direction, to a gate into a short lane between hedges just before the hamlet of Row. Turn right beyond the first house and then, a few metres further on, turn sharp left up the road. Take the track to the right and follow this beyond the last cottage where it continues between walls with fine views over the valley. At the junction with the path coming in from the left turn right and descend to the main road and the Lyth Valley Hotel.

Walk 5:
Potter Fell

Base point:	Hagg Foot - 1¹/₂m/2.5km east of Staveley
Map:	Outdoor Leisure - Lakes SE
Grid Reference:	SD 492979
Distance:	3¹/₂m/5.6km

Potter Fell is not the name given to any particular hill or summit: it is more an area of knolls, rocky outcrops and grassy hollows, a landscape of heather, bilberry, bracken and sheep-cropped turf with damp mosses, tiny becks, hidden waterfalls and bird-haunted tarns.

The walk starts at a footpath sign 200 metres west of Hagg Foot Farm on the Potter Fell Road between Garnett Bridge and Staveley, almost opposite Cockshot Wood. Parking may be found at several

Walk 5

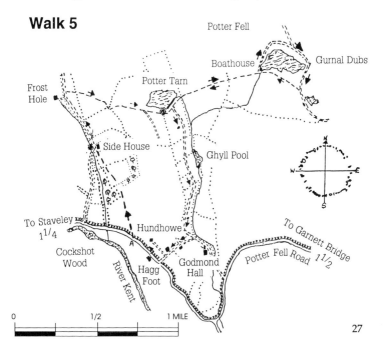

High Hundhowe (William Reading)

points along this stretch of the road.

Over the stile no path is visible across the field but the route goes up the slope diagonally bearing very slightly to the left. Once the top of the field is reached a track can be seen coming in from the right; join this close to the boundary wall of a wood on the left and continue through a gate to Side House, a cottage said to date from the thirteenth century, set in a wooded glen with a waterfall in the beck just below.

Beyond the barn a broad track runs straight ahead with a wall on the right and the beck below on the left. In a short distance Frost Hole can be seen in its hollow over on the left and by the gate above it is a footpath sign indicating the way to Potter Tarn by a narrow path up the fellside. Follow this, pass through gaps in the stone walls and continue forward along the track until it swings away to the right on the brow of the fell. At this point cross over the stile in the wall on the left by the tarn.

This stile has the best view of the Lakeland fells to be seen on this walk. Potter Tarn and its unsightly dam have few claims to beauty, especially in a dry season, but numbers of birds seem to find it attractive at certain times of the year. It is possible that at some future date it may be drained and the site made rather more appealing.

From the stile pass under the wall of the dam to the far side where a stile over the drystone wall leads to a good path up the fellside. In about ¼ mile climb a high stile to see, just below, a gem among tarns, set in a hollow among rocky knolls and surrounded by a sea of heather and bilberries and with a tiny tree-clad island near the north-west corner. Gurnal Dubs is a delight at all times but when the heather is in bloom and the scent is wafted on the breeze it has few rivals.

When time insists that you leave this scene return to Potter Tarn by the same route and from under the dam wall take the path which goes downhill directly away from the dam. This soon joins a broad track and passes by Ghyll Pool, another reservoir originally created for the papermills of James Cropper in the valley below. Continue down the track which, after a sharp hair-pin bend, is accompanied by the beck cascading in a deep gorge on the left, a spot bright with flowers in the spring and with berries in the autumn. Just beyond a pumphouse and just before Godmond Hall (a seventeenth-century house with an older pele tower attached), look for a gate on the right which leads into a very narrow bridleway and then into a lane, passing by an old byre and a substantial farmhouse to rejoin the road. Hagg Foot Farm and the starting point of the walk lie a few hundred metres along the road to the right.

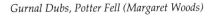

Gurnal Dubs, Potter Fell (Margaret Woods)

Walk 6:
Wet Sleddale

Base Point:	Car park by dam wall at Wet Sleddale Reservoir
Map:	Outdoor Leisure - Lakes NE
Grid Reference:	NY 555114
Distance:	3¹/₂m/5.6km

The M6 motorway, the A6 highway and the main west coast railway line all pass within a mile of the entrance to Wet Sleddale yet this is one of the most remote and least known of the valleys of Lakeland. Its isolation is ensured by the wide empty tracts of the Shap Fells to the south, Ralfland Forest to the north and Mosedale to the west, all approaches from these directions involving a long, dreary walk over lonely and uninspiring terrain. In itself Wet Sleddale has a special charm: walled pastures, scattered copses, ancient barns and farms, high-level bridleways and pleasant footpaths, swift-flowing becks, marshes bright with bog asphodel, butterwort and cotton grass, and, since the 1960s, a small artificial lake much loved by a variety of birds. The whole scene is watched

Packhorse Bridge and Falls, Wet Sleddale (William Reading)

30

Walk 6

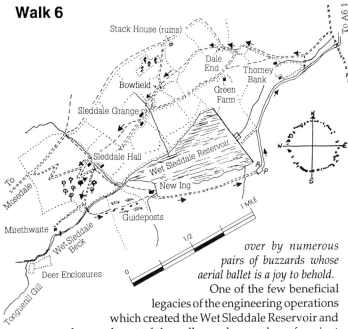

Stack House (ruins)

Dale
End

Thorney
Bank

Bowfield

Green
Farm

Sleddale Grange

Sleddale Hall

Wet Sleddale Reservoir

To
Mosedale

New Ing

1 MILE

Guideposts

Mirethwaite

Wet Sleddale Beck

½

To A6 1

Deer Enclosures

Tonguenil Gill

over by numerous
pairs of buzzards whose
aerial ballet is a joy to behold.

One of the few beneficial
legacies of the engineering operations
which created the Wet Sleddale Reservoir and
drowned part of the valley and a number of ancient
farmhouses is a useful car park just above the wall of the dam.
It is here that this walk begins.

The first stage involves a short walk back along the tarmac road
to a footbridge across the beck just beyond Cooper's Green,
approximately ½ mile from the car park. Cross the bridge to join
another road a few metres ahead. Turn left here, bear right by the
entrance to Thorney Bank and follow the road round the wall to the
gateway to Green Farm.

A track on the right near this gateway marks the beginning of
what is officially designated an unclassified road. There may well
have been such a highway here at one time but all that remains is a
damp hollow worn down by the passage of traffic long since
vanished, now a channel for any casual water and choked with
reeds. It is better to walk on the springy turf alongside for the short

31

Bog Asphodel (Peter Gambles)

distance to Dale End, a now half-derelict barn in an enclosure on the left. Until the end of the nineteenth century this was occupied as a farmhouse and shortly afterwards it was used as the school, the teacher living in a house now under the waters of the reservoir. The route goes through the gate to Dale End and then via the gate on the right into the field.

Cross the field towards a lone ash tree by a ruined wall, a direct line of less than 200 metres. Beyond this follow the wall and fence on the left, pass through another ruinous wall and then bear to the right up to the gate by the barn at Bowfield. Pass through the gates to a track on the right of the barn.

Like Dale End this, too, was lived in as a farmhouse until the early years of the twentieth century and as recently as the 1930s retained its seventeenth-century windows and fireplace. The pastures nearby have been identified as the site of the Common Field from the centuries before the enclosures took place.

Follow the track beyond Bowfield to Sleddale Grange, another historic building fallen from its former grandeur.

A photograph from 1936 shows a doorway here with a stone lintel carved with the date 1691 and the initials R M N but the records of Shap Abbey make it clear that long before this date this was, indeed, a "grange", belonging to the Abbey. In 1360 the Abbot complained that the grange had been illegally broken into and plundered, a transgression which carried spiritual as well as temporal penalties. The culprits were ordered by the Bishop to be "fully excommunicated with bell, book and candle", a severe punishment for the time.

A few metres beyond the stone building the path leaves the main track for a raised grassy level just above it on the right. Follow this on a course almost parallel to the track below to a stile in the wall

Cartmel Priory

over which the way lies straight ahead to Sleddale Hall, through a gate and across a tumbling beck.

Sleddale Hall is yet another of the many seventeenth-century farmhouses of Wet Sleddale which have fallen into ruin during recent times. It stands in a delightful position overlooking the valley and one suspects that but for the restrictions imposed by the Water Authority it would long ago have been made into a modern residence. The roof is still good; the rest is a sorry sight.

At the end of the house the route of this walk follows the broad track down to the left round the zig-zags and through the alder trees and on to the stone bridge over the Sleddale Beck. *(The bridleway straight ahead from Sleddale Hall is the long, lonely route to Mosedale, Swindale and Long Sleddale. From a point just above the Hall it is possible to see the ancient deer enclosures below by Sleddale Beck between Tonguerill Gill and Sherry Gill. These are unique in the Lake District.)*

At the bridge a white arrow indicates the next stage of the walk. This involves a passage over a stretch of marshy terrain where no path survives but the route to follow is shown by a line of white-topped guideposts which avoids the wetter parts. This should eventually lead directly to the ruins of New Ing, an old farmhouse near the end of the reservoir. From here a good, broad track goes straight to the car park, a pleasant stroll of about ³⁄₄ mile along the lake.

Buzzard (Sarah Mattocks)

Whitbarrow Scar

Walk 7:

Knipe Scar

Base Point:	Bampton Grange
Map:	Outdoor Leisure - Lakes NE
Grid Reference:	NY 524181
Distance:	4³⁄₄m/7.5km

This is a very pleasant walk following as close to the boundary of the National Park as the private land of the Lowther Estate permits. It includes a mile-long ramble at over 1000 feet along a limestone scar, Knipescar, a visit to the old hamlet of High Knipe and a stroll by the River Lowther. An abundant variety of birds and flowers and impressive views of the High Street fells add to the many pleasures of this delightful walk.

From Bampton Church follow the road eastwards through the village past the Crown and Mitre, noting the lovely old cottages, some of which bear dates from the early eighteenth century. Continue past the turning for Whale and Knipe and up the hill towards Shap. At the sharp bend in the road, about a mile from Bampton, turn left along a lane leading to Scarside Farm. Just beyond the farm the road becomes a track and soon leads to a gate which gives access to the open common.

Knipe Scar (William Reading)

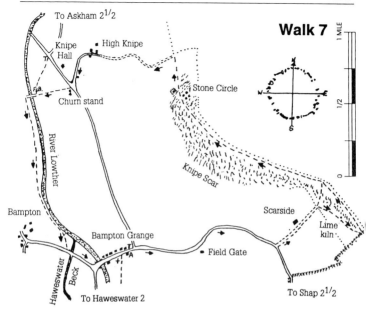

Walk 7

To Askham 2½

Knipe Hall • High Knipe

Stone Circle

Churn stand

River Lowther

Knipe Scar

Bampton

Scarside

Bampton Grange

Lime kiln

• Field Gate

Haweswater Beck

To Haweswater 2

To Shap 2½

Here the track bears slightly to the left and ascends to the wall at the top of the scar but an interesting alternative is to take the path to the right which passes by an old limekiln and then goes on to the plantation wall. Whichever choice is made turn left along the wall (noting the glimpse of Haweswater in the distance) and continue until the track begins to veer to the left and the wall turns round to the right near to an interesting and prominent limestone pavement. Straight ahead and just off the track is a prehistoric stone circle among naturally embedded rocks with a very large boulder in the centre, an ancient monument which it would be almost impossible to find without the aid of the notice indicating its presence. Return to the track and follow it (with Blencathra prominent in the distance) until it approaches a wall and turns sharply to the left to wind its way downhill to a gate and a narrow lane leading into the hamlet of High Knipe.

The farms and cottages here are all many hundreds of years old; Knipe Hall is of particular historical interest. The name derived from the Norse

River Lowther Suspension Bridge, High Knipe (William Reading)

word "gnipa" meaning rocky scar, and it seems likely that Knipe was originally a Norse farmstead.

On the common at the road junction is a local landmark, a substantial flat-topped milk stand, and from this point can be seen the footbridge across the river which is the next objective. Some will enjoy the swinging of the bridge as they cross; some will not; the former may pause to admire the dedication of the blissful pair who carved a lovers' heart in midstream; the latter will pause only when they reach the delightful greensward on the other side. Here follow a clear path, to the left, which hugs the river bank and follows it upstream all the way to the road bridge over the Haweswater Beck between Bampton and Bampton Grange.

Turn left towards Bampton Grange and in a short distance turn left again to cross the bridge over the River Lowther. Continue through the village past the school to the church and the Crown and Mitre.

St Patrick's Church at Bampton stands on the site of a chapel founded by the canons of Shap Abbey but the present church dates from 1726, with extensive and elegant alterations in the late Victorian period. Much of what we see today is little more than a century old but the artistic restraint and simplicity of an earlier age predominates.

Outstanding amongst the modern additions is the fine reredos of English oak inlaid with holly, and of the older furnishings perhaps those of greatest interest are the primitive Norman font and the seventeenth-

century parish chest. On the north wall hangs a portrait of John Bowstead, master of Bampton Grammar School for more than half a century and a renowned Latin scholar and teacher. From his tiny school, founded in 1623, many pupils went on to the universities and among Bampton's most famous men were Edmund Gibson, Bishop of Lincoln and London, Thomas Gibson, Physician-General to the armies of Marlborough, Hugh Curwen, Archbishop of Dublin and Bishop of Oxford (a sixteenth-century Vicar of Bray), Sir Charles Wilson, who became a judge, and Sir Charles Richardson, who became a Vice-Admiral. A local legend has it that in Bowstead's day even the plough-horses responded only to commands given in Latin. Many of the houses in Bampton are as old as the school but today there is no clamour from budding bishops nor stamp of learned horses to disturb its quiet village peace.

Walk 8:

Bampton Common and Haweswater

Base Point:	Naddle Gate - 1½m/2.5km south-west of Bampton Grange
Map:	Outdoor Leisure - Lakes NE
Grid Reference:	NY 511163
Distance:	4½m/7.3km

This walk begins near the dam which holds back the waters of the Haweswater Reservoir. It traverses the moors of Bampton Common with their strange and ruined relics of the ancient British folk who lived here more than 2000 years ago, descends beside the lovely gorge of the Measand Beck and ends along the shores of Haweswater. It is a walk of great variety, ideal for a fine, clear day but not recommended in mist.

At Naddle Gate a lane leaves the road from Bampton to Haweswater towards Burnbanks. Follow this as far as the first cottages and an old Manchester Waterworks signpost indicating the way to the footpath on the north-west shore of Haweswater. Take this track past the cottages and by a short zig-zag through the wood to a gate and stile. Continue for about 100 metres beyond the stile and turn very sharply right along a grassy track leading on to the fellside. Several other similar tracks will appear but keep to the

Walk 8

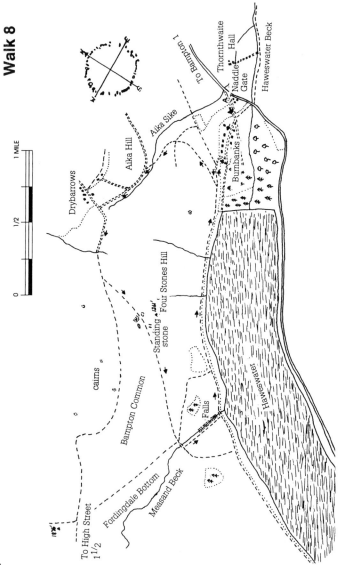

Bampton Grange (William Reading)

upper track always bearing left round the shoulder of the fell. At a crossing of tracks above Aika Sike continue on the same course round the fell until another track comes into view running at the foot of Aika Hill which is straight ahead. Cross the sike at any convenient point to join this track and follow it to the left. In about ¹/₂ mile the farmsteads at Drybarrows come into view and near the entrance to the farmyard a wide, grassy, tractor-rutted path on the left rises to the moorland of Bampton Common, the grazing ground of a handsome herd of black fell ponies.

Follow this path and shortly after passing a boggy patch (marked "Ford" on the map) a col is reached where the track divides. Take the lower route on the left and a fine view of Haweswater soon appears ahead. Aim for two standing stones with a small tarn nearby (unfortunately often dry) under Four Stones Hill which has three ancient cairns, one 36 feet in diameter and several feet high.

These now deserted moors above Haweswater were "home" to an unknown number of families in prehistoric times and scattered over the fellsides are the tumbled stones of their homesteads, bields, burial cairns, hut circles and, on Castle Crag, near the head of the lake is their fortress stronghold, strategically sited, and, like Dunmallet by Ullswater, a magnificent viewpoint.

From the standing stones the path goes steadily down to the footbridge over the Measand Beck now gathering force after its thousand foot descent from the High Street ridge. Cross the bridge and take the path down by the side of the beck towards the lakeshore. There is an "official" path a little way over to the right but it is more interesting to keep close to the beck and follow its course down. Below in the gorge cascades and waterfalls and deep pools abound, with a decorative fringe of rowan trees, silver birch, holly, gorse and seasonal flowers: a scene of sheer delight, the only sounds the splash of the water on the rocks and the cry of the birds over the moor or on the lake.

Descend to the lakeshore to join the broad path which extends along the entire length of this side of Haweswater. Follow this to the left and continue along it all the way back to the start of the walk at Burnbanks and Naddle Gate, an easy stroll of about 1¹/₂ miles.

Close to Naddle Gate is Thornthwaite Hall, a medieval pele tower, which has been identified with Vavasor Hall in Anthony Trollope's Palliser *novel,* Can You Forgive Her?, *although this is based on very slender evidence.*

Lapwing (Thomas Bewick)

40

Walk 9:
Moor Divock and Heughscar Hill

Base Point:	Askham
Map:	Outdoor Leisure - Lakes NE
Grid Reference:	NY 513237
Distance:	7m/11.25km

Askham is one of the most attractive villages in Westmorland. Its long main street, running down to the River Lowther, has a wide expanse of grass and trees, and on both sides are cottages and houses which together form an unusually charming architectural composition. Seventeenth- and eighteenth-century dates are carved into the stonework. The Queen's Head is a seventeenth-century inn once strategically situated on the main route from the west to the busy fairs and markets of Appleby. High above the river stands Askham Hall, now the home of the Lowther family whose former mansion, the great Gothic Lowther Castle, lies a spectacular ruin only a short distance away. Askham Hall is, outwardly, an Elizabethan country house but within it is a fourteenth-century pele tower. From 1375 to 1724 it was the Manor House of the Sandfords whose fortunes collapsed when they supported the losing side in the Civil War.

Ullswater from Heughscar (William Reading)

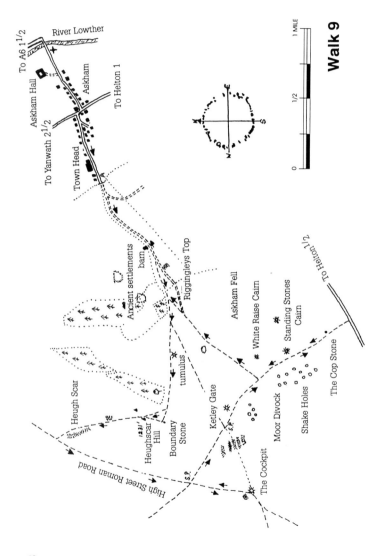

Walk 9

At the crossroads by the Queen's Head in Askham take the lane uphill and westwards (with the cul-de-sac sign). Keep to the right at the fork and proceed between houses, ancient and modern, to the cattle grid near Townhead Farm. Beyond this follow the track straight ahead keeping to the wall and ignoring all diversions to the left. Soon after passing the neat field-house at Howe Gill the track goes through a gate on to the open fell near the wood at Riggingleys Top.

The view to the east from this point encompasses the castle and church at Lowther and, beyond the M6, the extensive forest of Whinfell.

Through the gate a tempting path turns left: ignore this and keep along the wall on a gently rising route towards the corner of a walled plantation. Go alongside this and just beyond the end of the wall keep straight ahead to a boundary stone with an incised inscription which you may try to decipher. The summit cairn of Heughscar Hill is about 250 metres away to the right of this stone along a broad path of soft springy turf.

This is a splendid spot to enjoy a fine view of Ullswater with Helvellyn in the background, and far away to the east Cross Fell dominates the skyline.

From the summit cairn continue in the same direction among limestone outcrops and above Heughscar Crag on the left. At the end of the crag descend by an easy path to join a broad and well-worn track. This is High Street, the old Roman road. Turn to the left along this road and follow it to a crossroads junction of bridleways marked by a signpost. Continue forward along High Street for about 450 metres to the stone circle known as The Cockpit.

The Cockpit was a neolithic stone circle which, when complete. must have been an impressive structure. It appears to have consisted of two concentric circles, with inner and outer facing megaliths, and surrounded by an enclosing bank or wall. The internal diameter is about 85 feet (26 metres) and the external diameter probably about 120 feet (36 metres). We know almost nothing of the rituals and ceremonies which took place here but it was clearly a monument of some importance in the culture of the Bronze Age community who lived on Moor Divock 4000 years ago. Scattered along the route of this walk are stone circles, village settlements, tumuli and burial cairns from which cremated human remains, jet buttons and several primitively decorated food-vessels have been excavated, sparse

The Standing Stones, Moor Divock (CWAAS 1884-85)

relics of a long-vanished civilisation. Today we can only sit on what remains of this sanctuary and admire the discerning judgement of those who chose its site with its wonderful views of Ullswater and of the high fells and open countryside beyond.

To continue the walk return to the crossing of bridleways and the signpost.

Turn right here along the route pointing to Helton and proceed to Ketley Gate and another crossroads and signpost. (The Ordnance Map shows a bridleway direct from the Cockpit to Ketley Gate and the sign post confirms its reputed existence: in its present state it is not recommended to walkers as it is made hazardous by a bog which may be neither negotiated nor circumvented without a high degree of risk, frustration and athleticism. The recommended route is pleasanter, safer and only 400 metres longer.)

At Ketley Gate continue along the path towards Helton and enjoy an easy stroll for $^3/_4$ mile as far as the Cop Stone, passing on the way a number of ruined burial cairns, the most interesting of which is White Raise, a few yards off the path on the left, which still retains the carefully constructed stone kist in which the cremation vessel was placed.

The Cop Stone is an isolated megalith almost five feet high, the lone survivor of a stone circle once enclosed within a stone bank the outline of which may just be traced.

From the Cop Stone return along the bridleway for a short distance to visit the Standing Stones just off the track on the right-hand side.

The Standing Stones are the remains of an impressive burial cairn within a circle of large upright stones. A food-vessel decorated with a rope motif was recovered from this burial together with a number of human bones.

Return to the main bridleway and in approximately 300 metres take the track off to the right which leads directly across the moor to the fell gate at Riggingleys Top and the way back to Askham.

Fell Pony (Jennifer Buxton [from The Fell Pony *by Clive Richardson: J.A.Allen 1990])*

Walk 10:
Dacre and Hutton John

Base Point:	Dacre Church
Map:	Outdoor Leisure - Lakes NE
Grid Reference:	NY 460266
Distance:	3³/₄m/6km

Dacre lies less than two miles from the meeting point of two major historic routes running north-south and east-west. These routes are now designated as the A6 and the A66 but throughout the history of England they have been of strategic importance. It seemed appropriate, therefore, that in the summer of 927 the Kings of England, Scotland, Strathclyde and Dyfed should foregather here to hold what to-day we should call a summit conference, the main purpose of which was to establish Athelstan of England's overlordship in Britain. Tradition has it that the monastery at Dacre was the setting for this great meeting of kings and even if the Treaty proved to be very short-lived the occasion gave Dacre its place in the history

Church and Castle, Dacre (William Reading)

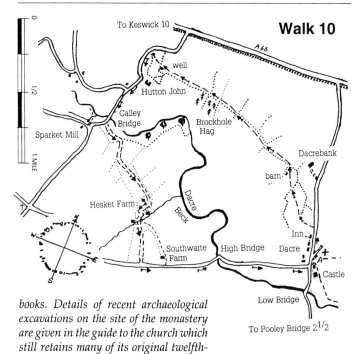

Walk 10

To Keswick 10

A 66

well

Hutton John

Calley
Bridge

Brockhole
Hag

Sparket Mill

Dacrebank

barn

Dacre Beck

Hesket Farm

Beck

Inn

Southwaite
Farm

High Bridge

Dacre

Castle

Low Bridge

To Pooley Bridge 2½

books. *Details of recent archaeological excavations on the site of the monastery are given in the guide to the church which still retains many of its original twelfth-century features and also has two cross-shafts from the ninth and tenth centuries carved with the figures of Adam and Eve and various animals.*

The four corners of the original churchyard are marked by stone figures of the Dacre Bears. These appear to tell the story of one bear who is first seen to the north-west of the church squatting against a pillar; to the south-west he is jumped on by a lynx and is raising his head; to the south-east he is reaching with his paw over his shoulder to try to seize the attacker; to the north-east the bear is alone again with a satisfied smile on his face. All the figures are weather-worn and some imagination is needed to follow these events!

Dacre Castle is a fourteenth-century pele tower which has retained its medieval appearance, unlike those at Muncaster, Dalemain and Askham which have been buried in later mansions. It is extremely well preserved both externally and internally. The present elegant domesticity of the

47

interior contrasts sharply with the account given in 1802 which commented on "the gloom which over spreads the interior" and felt it to be "truly expressive of the dark ages of medieval tyranny".

The Castle may be visited but only by prior arrangement.

To begin the walk return to the road through the village and turn right up the hill past the old school and the Horse and Farrier Inn. Just beyond the last building on the left is a stile and a gap in the hedge. The path goes straight across the first field to a gap in the next hedge then bears diagonally uphill to a tall stile between trees. From here the path continues diagonally, leaving a small field house on the left, to a large stone stile in the corner.

Over the stile turn left along the track from Dacre Bank Farm to a gate. Beyond this the path follows the fence, changing sides at the first zig-zag so that it passes on the uphill side of the small, steep wood called Brockhole Hag. Beyond the wood the view across the valley towards the Dacre Beck is enhanced by an interesting variety of tree species, planted no doubt to give pleasure to the inhabitants of the house at Hutton John. The elegant pineapple-topped gateposts here suggest that this may once have been part of a "Ladies' Walk" in the grounds of the mansion.

Hutton John is built round a fourteenth-century pele tower which retains most of its original features. Much of the rest of the house is of seventeenth-century construction and there is also some Elizabethan panelling, an eighteenth-century staircase and plaster ceiling, and the usual Victorian additions such as the library and imposing entrance hall. Ownership passed from the Huttons to the Hudlestons in 1564 and still remains in their hands as a private house, not open to the public.

Just before the splendid old barn there is a tall, strangely formed rubbing post near the drinking troughs and the now covered "St Mary's Well" in the corner. The path goes straight on across one field to join the road on Hawbrow.

Turn left down the lane known as Hawbrow and continue past the main gate of Hutton John bearing left at the junction and on to Calley Bridge over the Dacre Beck.

Across the bridge the route goes left through a gate, but before proceeding it is worthwhile making a few minutes detour to see the mill at Sparket where the water-wheel is driven by a head of water from a small mill pool which is fed by a mill-race seen winding its way across the field. A

Hutton John (William Reading)

cluster of picturesque cottages stands in a hollow where several fast-flowing watercourses meet.

To continue the walk return towards the bridge and take the path on the right which goes across the fields to Hesket Farm. There is a clear route past the farmhouse, through the buildings and down to the bridge. But the footpath leaves the farm drive on the left just before the bridge and takes a footbridge across Greaves Beck and straight ahead towards Southwaite Farm where signs direct it around the farmyard and on to the road. This path can be extremely muddy so the Hesket Farm drive can be a better alternative.

Turn left along the road down to High Bridge. Here the Dacre Beck cuts deep into the sedimentary rock as it swirls under the bridge. Continue to the road junction in Dacre village; turn left to return to the church and the start of the walk.

Walk 11:
Greystoke

Base Point:	Coachgate - off A66, 4¹/₂m/7.3km west of M6 at Penrith
Map:	Pathfinder NY 43/53 & Outdoor Leisure - Lakes NW
Grid Reference:	NY 439278
Distance:	7¹/₄m/11.7km

The boundary of the National Park here is the line of the old railway so, apart from the short distance along Crag Lonning, this walk makes a loop out of the Park. It visits the ancient villages of Penruddock, Motherby, Greystoke and Greystoke Gill and on a good day the views of the Lakeland fells and the Pennines are splendid.

Coachgate is the name given to the road leading straight to Greystoke from the present A66. There is usually space to park here.

The walk begins by turning off Coachgate into a green lane known as Crag Lonning which runs parallel to the disused railway track. In summer the pale blue spikes of giant bellflower grow abundantly on the limestone here.

Greystoke Castle, entrance gate (William Reading)

Walk 11

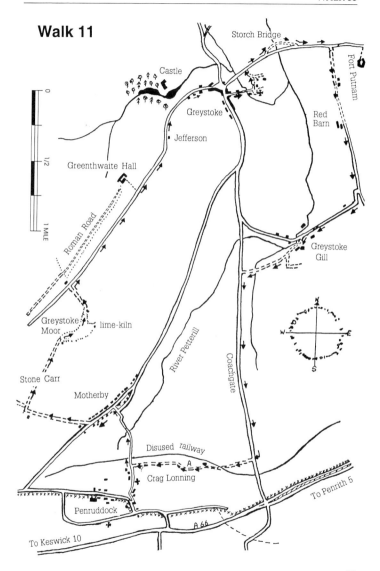

Castle

Storch Bridge

Fort Putnam

Greystoke

Red Barn

Jefferson

Greenthwaite Hall

Roman Road

Greystoke Gill

Greystoke Moor

lime-kiln

Stone Carr

River Petterill

Coachgate

Motherby

Disused *railway*

Crag Lonning

A

Penruddock

To Penrith 5

A 66

To Keswick 10

Greystoke Castle (Margaret Woods)

Crag Lonning emerges on to the road among the old houses at Penruddock. Turn right and after passing through the line of the railway cross over the infant River Petteril at Brigbeck. The road winds its way between substantial stone walls up to Motherby. Turn left at the junction and walk along the street noting the ornate dated lintels on some of the houses. Just before the petrol station turn right along the bridleway signposted to Greystoke Moor. On a clear day the views are spectacular, with Blencathra dominating the scene.

In about ½ mile the bridleway takes a sharp right turn but before proceeding along it spare time to climb over the stile on the left and to walk to the top of the rising ground ahead.

Called Stone Carr this is a mysterious place of banks and ditches with more recent walls crossing them and may be on the route of a Roman road. Aerial photography has identified the site just north-east of here as a Roman camp.

In more recent times this was the arena for the annual Greystoke Sports, referred to in James Clarke's 1789 Survey of the Lakes *as a place where "time out of mind races and other sports were held - wrestling, leaping and tracing with dogs". When the curlew call on a morning in spring or the snipe drum here in the evening this is a place of magic and mystery.*

Return to the bridleway and follow it to the top of Greystoke Moor, land which was open moorland until it was enclosed and drained for agriculture in 1812. The limekiln in the field on the right was used for on-the-spot limeburning to improve the soil. The path keeps close to the wall on the left as it passes through an area of overgrown quarries much loved by rabbits and known as "Sam's Cabin". There are good views towards Cross Fell over the Eden Valley before the route rejoins the lane and meets the Berrier road opposite Greystoke Moor Cottage.

Turn right along this road which runs parallel with the line of the Roman road behind the wall one field away to the left.

This tall wall was built by the Duke of Norfolk when he bought up several of the estates around the already extensive lands of Greystoke Park in the late eighteenth century. Greenthwaite Hall, built by Miles Halton in 1650, was one such estate and appears as the next farmhouse on the left, notable for its multi-storied porch which faces towards the old road.

Continue down the road to catch a fleeting glimpse of the handsome castle of Greystoke.

This was described by Nicholas Pevsner as "an ambitious and correct neo-Elizabethan mansion by Salvin" built mainly in the 1840s, but hidden away is an ancient fourteenth-century pele tower with massive medieval masonry. It has been a home of the Howard family since 1569 and, except for special events, it is not normally open to the public.

The picturesque centre of Greystoke has an old cross near the arched entrance to the castle. From here follow the road round to the right past the Boot and Shoe Inn and then turn left by the post office

The Sanctuary Stone, Greystoke (Margaret Woods)

53

into Church Road and so on to the church.

Many of the stone buildings bear the date of construction and the Howard initials. The bridge in this road was first built by the Duke and renovated soon after the First World War as a war memorial. Enclosed in iron rails near the swimming pool is the Sanctuary Stone which marked the boundary of the area round the church to which those seeking sanctuary from the law could flee, a dispensation which was brought to an end by Henry VIII who considered this privilege to be an abuse of his authority.

The Church of St Andrew is unusually large for a small village and this is explained by the arrival here, probably in the thirteenth century, of a group of Augustinian Canons. Within the Church were built six chantry chapels with priests to pray for the souls of the dead and in due course a College was established to teach boys from the locality. This was also ended by the events of Henry VIII's reign and so Greystoke was perhaps deprived of a great opportunity to create a northern rival to the College at Eton, which was founded in a similar manner. More fascinating details may be read in the church guide.

From the Church walk in a northerly direction past Church House, through the gate and along the path towards the Rectory. Halfway along this field path is a small stone, with a scooped-out hollow, called the Plague Stone, traditionally the spot where plague victims placed their payments for food in a pool of vinegar.

Fort Putnam, Greystoke (Margaret Woods)

At the next gate turn left down the drive and then turn right along the main Penrith road for about ¹/₂ mile. Much of this distance can be covered off the road by taking the loop of the old road which crosses the River Petteril by the old Storch Bridge.

Turn right at the next junction over a cattle grid along a road leading to Red Barn.

The "fortress" up on the left is a farm built by the Duke of Norfolk in 1778. It is known as Fort Putnam and is one of the eccentric follies he created here. Bunkers Hill may be seen further up the hill and Spire House is about ¹/₂ mile away in the direction of Blencowe. These are all monuments to one man's personal fantasy but they are not without architectural merit.

Beyond the gated track to Red Barn continue down the metalled road and turn right at the junction towards Greystoke Gill. From this road there are good views along the shallow valley towards Greystoke Church.

Greystoke Gill is a pretty little hamlet with the River Petteril wandering across the road. Turn left before crossing the river and follow the path between the farm buildings and the river. At the division in the path keep right. The way gets narrower because the hedges have become overgrown but persevere because this is a very old path.

It is said that if you count the species of shrubs growing in 100 yards of hedge then multiply that figure by 100 you have an indication of the age of the hedge.

At the end of the lane turn left and out onto Coachgate once again. It is just a mile to the old railway and quite flat, so a pleasant walk back between fields and hedgerows to the starting point.

Greystoke Church (Margaret Woods)

55

Walk 12:
Castle How and Newlands Mill

Base point:	Millhouse - 1¹/₂m/2.5km south east of Hesket Newmarket
Map:	Pathfinder NY 23/33
Grid Reference:	NY 363376
Distance:	3³/₄m/6km

This walk combines the very old with the very new. Castle How is an ancient hill fort from which the parish of Castle Sowerby derives its name. It has associations with the Red Knights, a force of mounted men whose duty it was to uphold the rights of the Lord of the Forest of Inglewood and to repel any raiders. Their Staff of Office was a nine-foot-long red spear much revered in the locality. Once a year, at Whit, at the opening of the Penrith Fair, the Red Knights would assemble in a show of force when they rode through the streets of Penrith brandishing their spears and shouting defiance to any who should dispute the title of their Lord. Little remained even 150 years ago, of the defensive structure where tenants and stock could retreat during the border raids but the wide track is still visible as well as banks and ditches amongst the trees.

Newlands Windmills are modern structures, of the new breed of electricity generators intended to be more "environmentally friendly" than those which burn fossil fuels. The huge rotors are certainly spectacular as they turn in the breeze with an impressive swoosh.

Castle How (William Reading)

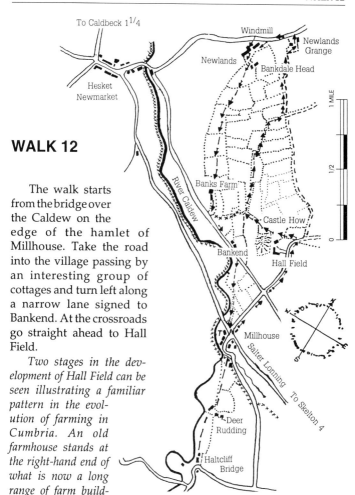

WALK 12

The walk starts from the bridge over the Caldew on the edge of the hamlet of Millhouse. Take the road into the village passing by an interesting group of cottages and turn left along a narrow lane signed to Bankend. At the crossroads go straight ahead to Hall Field.

Two stages in the development of Hall Field can be seen illustrating a familiar pattern in the evolution of farming in Cumbria. An old farmhouse stands at the right-hand end of what is now a long range of farm buildings, its presence given away by the small blocked-up windows. The more recent and elegant white farmhouse which stands back away from the farmyard would have been built in the prosperous days of the late seventeenth and early eighteenth centuries.

Pass by the entrance to Hall Field Farm and at the gate turn left and follow the track down past the end of the house and on up the field onto the ridge. The remains of Castle How lie in the trees to the left with clear views for the watchmen across the Solway Plain to the right.

A tall stile can be seen taking the path on and down the other side of the How. Keep the hedge on the right until a meeting of tracks near an old limekiln, no doubt used when these fields were first enclosed and improved.

The route continues through a gate almost opposite the path from Castle How. Follow the hedge on the right to a gate then follow the hedge on the left up to a stile, beyond which the real path is rather lost but follow the right-hand boundary until the gate and track come into view beneath tall sycamore trees. Once at the gate the deeply rutted path leaves no doubt as to its direction and continues to a second gate at the corner and on down a fenced track with a tall hedge on the left and the first close views of one of the windmills (or wind driven generators) looming over the hill on the left.

About half way down this short fenced track turn left through a rather tumbled-down gate and cross this first field. This is the almost lost bridleway which has come straight across the fields from Hall Field. Looking back you can see the old gates. From here the route follows the hedge on the right and passes through a series of good gates to the farm at Newlands Grange.

This is a countryside of tall hedges live with the chink of tits in spring and providing food for hordes of fieldfares in the autumn.

As Newlands Grange is approached turn right through a gate into a field at the back of the farmhouse and keep on round to the right to find a small gate on to the drive between the house yard and the farm buildings. Once on the road turn left towards the cornmill.

Turn left at the wide entrance to the mill and with one windmill and mill buildings on the right follow the road up to a gate where a road can be seen winding its way up a field to the second windmill. The old public right of way was further left but following the new road is easier and acceptable to the landowner.

Standing beneath the windmill is breathtaking.

The original stile is right by the windmill and takes the path on along the ridge with views of the Caldbeck Fells and Blencathra to the south. Cross the line of an ancient hedge marked now by a sad row of windswept hawthorns and keep the fence on the left until the next stile. Two more fields now remain to be crossed before the path passes through the yard at Banks Farm and down to the road. Turn left towards the farm at Bankend. Just beyond the farm, on the opposite side of the road, is the start of a pleasant riverside route back to the bridge at Millhouse, a right of way but not very clearly marked.

Newlands Windmill (William Reading)

Walk 13:
Watersmeet and the Howk

Base Point:	Hesket Newmarket
Map:	Pathfinder NY 23/33
Grid Reference:	NY 341387
Distance:	5m/8km

Starting from the wide street of the old market town of Hesket Newmarket we follow the course of the River Caldew through pleasant woodland to the strangely mysterious peninsula where it joins the Cald Beck at the appropriately named "Watersmeet". A path by the beck takes us through more flower-bedecked woodlands to the little town of Caldbeck, once a bustling centre of industry and, of course, home to John Peel. There is much of interest here. The furthest point of the walk is the deep limestone gorge known as The Howk with its ruined bobbin mill and the waters of the Cald Beck roaring below.

From the centre of Hesket Newmarket follow a sign opposite the Old Crown Inn, towards Caldbeck and Sebergham.

It should be noted that the first part of this path is not the same as the one on the OS map but has recently been altered.

After crossing the first field to a gate turn right into a fenced path, then at the next gate follow the yellow waymark to the left. Keeping the hedge on the left, you wind down towards the Caldew again and into a wood. The path keeps high up the bank in the deciduous woodland, and with dappled sunlight, the sound and sight of the river, the seasonal flowers and perhaps the song of a wren this turns out to be one of the many magical places on this walk.

From the wood follow the guide posts leading across the field cutting off a wide wooded meander of the river and crossing a farm track. Ancient hawthorns funnel the path to a kissing-gate into riverbank woodland again, where some of the old trees have been coppiced, then out into a meadow which in June has a remarkable variety of flowers.

At this point the course of the rivers becomes very interesting. The

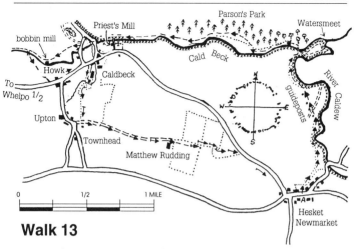

Walk 13

River Caldew is on the right, and approaching from the left the Cald Beck almost joins it, but, at the last minute, careers off under the footbridge and along a narrow gorge cut through the sandstone, leaving a narrow isthmus of land, which widens out into a wooded peninsula known as Watersmeet.

Our route turns left over the footbridge but if time allows it is worth following the circular path around the peninsula to take your leave of the Caldew.

From the bridge follow the Cald Beck upstream and, where the second field narrows, a stile on the right takes the path up through a break in the coniferous woodland known as Parson's Park where in summer the clearings are full of foxgloves and butterflies. The path soon joins the beck again and follows it into the village of Caldbeck.

The first mill to be seen on the left is Priest's Mill, an eighteenth-century watermill, where in the season there are several small shops, a mining museum and a cafe which can all be reached by crossing the little bridge near the church.

The mill is open from 10.30am to 5pm, every day except Monday from mid March to 31st October, also open on bank holidays, and Saturdays and Sundays in November and December.

The ancient church at Caldbeck is dedicated to St Kentigern, a Scot whose childhood name was Mungo and tradition has it that he baptised the

61

Priest's Mill, Caldbeck (William Reading)

first Christians of the village here in the sixth century. Nowadays, children are still brought to be accepted into the Christian family at St Mungo's Well, beside the little arched bridge which crosses from the church to Friar Row.

Early in the twelfth century the area around Caldbeck had such a reputation for being a wild place, frequented by rogues and vagabonds, that a licence was granted to the Prior of Carlisle, by the Chief Forester of Inglewood, to build a hospice for the relief of distressed travellers, probably on the site now occupied by the Rectory, next to the Church. The monks who ran the hospice probably lived in the vicinity of Friar Row.

Caldbeck seems now to be a quiet place but in Elizabethan times there was a saying,

> "Caldbeck and Caldbeck Fells
> Are worth all England else".

This was when the silver, lead and copper mines up on the fells were producing wealth for the country, though very little of this, apart from a meagre livelihood for the miners and those providing the necessary services, seems to have stayed in the area. There is no evidence today of the great wealth which passed through.

The village itself must have been a very noisy, bustling place in the *eighteenth and nineteenth centuries and there is plenty of evidence to be found of the old industries. As many as eight mills rumbled and clattered, powered by the obliging waters of the Cald Beck and its tributaries. Priest's Mill had been built as a corn mill but later became a saw mill. Downstream there was a papermill and upstream a woollen mill which wove the grey wool from the local herdwick sheep into cloth before the fulling mills completed the process, making a firm close-textured waterproof fabric. This was the "Hodden Grey" cloth made famous as the "coat so grey" of John Peel who hunted hereabouts and whose grave is marked by an appropriately carved white stone in the churchyard.*

In the Howk, a limestone gorge west of the village, the Cald Beck powered a bobbin mill newly built in 1857 and ceasing production in 1920 with the decline in the textile industry but then gutted by fire in the 1950s.

The nineteenth century was the time when Caldbeck was at its busiest. In the 1850s there were 1500 people here but by the early twentieth century the population of Caldbeck had dropped to 600. Everything came together - the economic life of the mines came to an end, the textile industry suffered from competition from the bigger concerns in the industrial towns, the bobbin mills suffered from the decline in the local need for bobbins, from cheap imports and later of course from plastic bobbins. All this reduced the service industries: there were no pit ponies to be shod by the blacksmiths or heavy mine equipment to be forged, no arching to be done by the stonemasons, not so much work for cloggers, shoemakers or tailors and less trade for the butchers, millers and brewers. In a self-sufficient community like this everything was interdependent and once the industries closed the craftsmen moved on to find work elsewhere leaving the farming community to manage the land.

We arrived in Caldbeck along the lane from Parson's Park and the next stage of the walk carries on in the same direction leaving the footbridge by the church on the left, past Friar Hall and along Friar Row to the junction with the main road. Cross the road into the car park by the Cald Beck and following the car exit route bear right up the bank, emerging on to the green by the village pond, known locally as Claydubs, where a great variety of waterfowl, including some immaculate mandarin ducks, enjoy being fed by their many visitors.

The next stage of the walk takes us to The Howk, the name given to the deep limestone gorge with the ruins of a great bobbin mill.

Bobbin Mill, The Howk, Caldbeck (William Reading)

The entrance to the gorge is not at first easily seen: on the west side of the pond just above the bridge by the old brewery look for a large wooden door between the buildings. This has a small wicket gate and a sign pointing to "The Howk": it all looks very private but once through the door the path onwards is clear. Follow it along the gorge and in less than ¼ mile the ruins of the mill will be seen.

The neglected bobbin mill occupies the widest part of the gorge. The tall barn-like building was the drying shed for the coppice timber before it was processed and the main mill stands on the very edge of the cliff, with some remaining charred timbers from the 1958 fire. Red Rover, the huge water-wheel which provided the power for the mill turned in a pit at the far end of the building, its water being piped from a higher pool.

The only path winds its way on past the mill, rising above the beck, up steps in the rocky cliff side. At times it is not possible to see the water but it can always be heard especially after a storm when the deep gulley amplifies its roar.

At the top of the gorge a footbridge provides a fine view of the foaming waters below. Cross the bridge and follow the path bearing left around the field back to the roadside stile. Go left along the road passing the farm at Todcroft on the left and then turn right towards Upton.

Askham village green
Bassenthwaite Lake

Isel
Crummock Water

The stone building which stands on the green in the middle of this junction was once the school; its modern counterpart is just across the road.

Follow the road as it winds through Upton, an interesting group of old and modern houses, and just after it has passed over a picturesque bridge over Gill Beck turn left at Townhead up the farm drive to Matthew Rudding.

A stile, easily seen from the yard gate, takes the path from the front of the farmhouse to the far left-hand corner of the first field. Cross the hedge on the left here and then continue on in the same direction with the hedge on the right to a stile into an L-shaped field. Aim for a stile at the right-hand end of the road-side boundary.

At the road turn right and after a short distance, mostly downhill, re-enter Hesket Newmarket.

The unusual building on the left at the edge of the village is a seventeenth-century Hall and was noted by Daniel and Samuel Lysons as having "twelve angles and a circular roof so contrived that the shadows give the hours of the day" (Magna Britannia 1816).

Walk 14:
Bassenthwaite Lake and Dodd Wood

Base Point:	The Old Saw Mill, Dodd Wood - on the A591, 4m/6.5km north-east of Keswick
Map:	Outdoor Leisure - Lakes NW
Grid Reference:	NY 235282
Distance:	6m/9.7km (or two separate walks of 3m/4.8km)

This is an easy and varied walk, quite undemanding - except for the short (optional) climb to the summit of Dodd - and passing through contrasting scenery with fine viewpoints and many features of widely different interest. There are few short walks on which it is possible to combine a tour of one of the oldest national forests in the country with a visit to an eighteenth-century country house and a tenth-century church, and for good measure a stroll beside a lake which inspired Tennyson to write the most dramatic lines of Morte d'Arthur. *Bassenthwaite Lake is, perhaps, the least appreciated of all the lakes - indeed, it is, strictly speaking, the only*

Walk 14

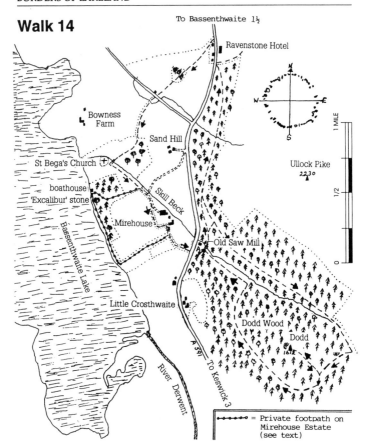

To Bassenthwaite 1½

Ravenstone Hotel

N

W — E

S

1 MILE

1/2

0

Bowness Farm

Sand Hill

Ullock Pike
2230
▲

St Bega's Church ✝

boathouse

'Excalibur' stone

Skill Beck

Mirehouse

Bassenthwaite Lake

Old Saw Mill

Little Crosthwaite

Dodd Wood

Dodd

A 591

To Keswick 3

River Derwent

●━●━●━● = Private footpath on
          Mirehouse Estate
          (see text)

lake. It lacks the mountain spectacle of Wastwater, Ullswater or Ennerdale Water, and cannot match the jewelled charm of Grasmere, Esthwaite or Rydal Water, and consequently, as Mrs Lynn Linton commented in 1864, "Poor Bassenthwaite scarcely gets its due.....few people see the sweetness which would have charmed many but for the blinding power of contrast." Those who venture on the walk described here will surely discover something of this sweetness and charm.

NOTE: *In order to visit Mirehouse and to walk along the shoreline*

66

path (which is on the private land of the Mirehouse estate) it is necessary to purchase the appropriate tickets at the Old Saw Mill before starting the walk. These tickets are available only at times when the house itself is open to the public - that is, from the beginning of April to the end of October, daily from 10.30 - 5.30. At other times this part of the route is not available and only the public right of way should be used.

The walk starts from the Old Saw Mill where there is a car park and tea room.

Cross the footbridge behind the tea room and go first right and then left on the rising path, negotiating a hair-pin bend in order to reach the forest road. This is a good level footpath which continues well above and almost parallel to the road below. Follow this straight ahead among a pleasant mixture of imposing conifers and deciduous broadleaves with views over the pastures and woodlands to the lake.

In just under a mile the path descends to the road near the Ravenstone Hotel. Join the road, which can be busy in the summer season, and 200 metres ahead by Ravenstone Lodge on the left, look for a Public Footpath sign. This leads down a set of steps to a clear path, at first close to the cottages and then across meadows by a group of fine pine trees to a kissing gate with a causeway beyond it.

Bear slightly left along the causeway to a stile. After this continue for about 1/2 mile through a series of kissing gates across fields and through small woodlands to a lane. Cross straight over the lane to a gate and a broad track which goes along a wall and through

St Bega's Church, Bassenthwaite (William Reading)

67

delightful parkland inclining gently towards the lake and notable for a number of very fine trees. The little church will be seen by the lake shore.

The exterior architecture of St Bega's Church is clearly Victorian with no particularly distinguishing features but the interior reveals a long and fascinating history. The chancel and nave, which formed the original church, are almost certainly of the tenth century which would suggest a date to coincide with the period of Norse settlement. The arch between the chancel and the south transept is probably twelfth-century and the arch in the south aisle itself dates from the foundation of the chantry chapel in the fourteenth century. Attached to the south pillar of the chancel arch is a wrought iron hour glass, probably Elizabethan, which enabled the congregation to keep a check on the length of the sermon. Many a learned priest must have eyed this apprehensively and recalled the words of the poet, Horace, "Breve esse labora, obscurus fio", ie. "When I am struggling to be brief I become unintelligible".

The strangely isolated site of the church today may be explained by the fact that in former days most worshippers would travel to St Bega's by water rather than by land. An ancient causeway used to exist along the lake shore passing by the church but this would serve only a small part of the local population.

Little is known of St Bega other than that she was the daughter of an Irish chieftain and her religious commitment was such that she fled from Ireland in order to avoid a forced marriage to a Norseman chosen for her by her father. She entered the Priory at St Bees in the seventh century. There is no evidence to lend support to the legend that the church by Bassenthwaite Lake marks her place of burial.

There can be few churches so perfectly situated for prayer and quiet meditation.

To continue the walk retrace your steps from the church for the few metres to the Skill Beck. Turn right along the course of the beck and follow the path to the boundary fence near to Mirehouse.

IF YOU HAVE OBTAINED TICKETS FOR MIREHOUSE YOU SHOULD TURN RIGHT AT THIS POINT TO WALK ALONG THE FENCE AND ENTER CASTOCKS WOOD TO REACH THE SHORE OF THE LAKE. NEAR THE BOATHOUSE IS A SHORT STONE COLUMN WITH A PLAQUE BEARING THE FAMOUS LINES FROM TENNYSON'S *MORTE D'ARTHUR* TELLING THE STORY

OF KING ARTHUR'S SWORD "EXCALIBUR". FROM HERE FOLLOW THE PATH ALONG THE SHORE AND BACK TO THE HOUSE AS INDICATED ON THE MAP. A VISIT TO THE HOUSE CAN BE RECOMMENDED.

If you have not purchased a permit for the lakeside path you should continue straight ahead along the public right of way in front of the house and follow it round and back to the road.

The Old Saw Mill and the car park are on the opposite side of the road.

This completes the first section of the walk and, in the summer season, the refreshment room may provide a welcome pause before embarking on the more strenuous tour of Dodd Wood. This may, of course, be enjoyed as a quite separate three mile walk for another occasion.

The route through the wood is indicated on the accompanying map and also on a large-scale map fixed to the wall of the Saw Mill. Far better than either of these is the Forestry Commission's guide to Dodd Wood which may be obtained for a few pence from the shop at the Saw Mill or, out of season, from the local office at Peil Wyke, Bassenthwaite Lake, near Cockermouth, Cumbria CA13 9YQ.

Dodd Wood is part of the North Lakes Forest, the oldest forest in the Lake District. The medieval woodlands of natural broadleaved trees were largely cleared for charcoal manufacture and subsequent sheep grazing prevented regeneration. Many landowners in the eighteenth century foresaw the danger of a national shortage of timber and began to plant fast-

growing conifers, a development which was roundly condemned by William Wordsworth as turning the natural landscape into a "vegetable manufactory", but which has now become accepted as part of the varied Lakeland scene. Among those who began the plantations was Thomas Story of Mirehouse. Near the car park are some of the trees he planted - silver firs, Scots pines and European larches, now very large and impressive. Since 1919 the Forestry Commission has

European larch (Peter Gambles)

69

Norway spruce (Sylvia Rigby)

further developed Dodd Wood and in recent decades has undertaken a programme of sensitive landscaping.

In the course of the walk a great variety of tree species may be identified. These include, in addition to those referred to above, Sitka spruce, Japanese larch, Douglas firs up 30 metres in height, western hemlock, oak, beech, rowan, hazel and silver birch. Many birds and animals frequent the wood, among them the red squirrel, badgers, roe deer, the rare pine marten and the tawny owl.

The reward for the short climb to the summit of Dodd is, on a clear day, a wide vista of the Lakeland fells extending from Helvellyn to Scafell Pike and on to Grisedale Pike and the white "Bishop" stone on Barf, with the Solway Firth and the Scottish hills yet further away.

The full tour of Dodd Wood is along good paths and forest roadways with easy gradients and at a leisurely pace takes about 2½ hours.

Walk 15:
Isel, Blindcrake and Sunderland

Base Point:	Isel Bridge - 3m/4.8km north-east of Cockermouth
Map:	Pathfinder NY 03/13
Grid Reference:	NY 164333
Distance:	5½m/9km

This walk is best begun by a visit to Isel Church, an interesting Norman structure still retaining many of its twelfth century features and with a delightful riverside churchyard perhaps seen at its glorious best in its spring display of snowdrops, aconites and

Walk 15

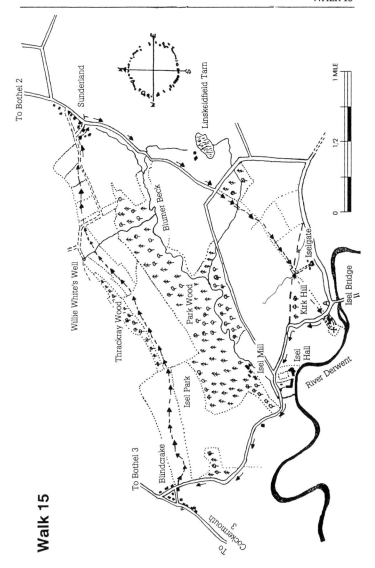

Blindcrake (William Reading)

primroses but having a wide variety of wild flowers summer long.

From Isel Bridge take the road northwards towards Isel Hall and Blindcrake. The Hall is seen standing high above the river across the fields to the left, and in about ¹/₂ mile, after passing by a group of elegant old almshouses and a sharp left turn, the road goes by the Hall's "armed" gates.

Isel Hall is a spectacular sixteenth-century mansion built round a medieval pele tower. It retains some features constructed in the reign of Henry VIII notably several imposing fireplaces. There is also some splendid linenfold panelling and much of the Elizabethan panelling has decorative inlay of the kind known as Italian intarsia. It was for many generations the home of the Lawson family who were not universally beloved in their county, having acquired a reputation as overbearing and rapacious landlords. The Hall is not open to the public. Isel Mill stands opposite the Hall on Blumer Beck which joins the Derwent a little further along the road among fields where creamy Charolais cattle graze.

The road now gradually rises for nearly a mile and on the way it is interesting to note that in 1836 this remote settlement provided a finely built school for the education of its children, an example of that concern for education which gave Cumberland and Westmorland the highest standard in the country at that time. Beyond the "school", now a house, the road rises to give wide views over the valley and towards Skiddaw, and in a short distance reaches the hamlet of Blindcrake.

Opposite the first house, which used to be the Ghyll Yeat Public House, is a footpath sign to "Sunderland". Follow this track as it winds its way up the rough land on to Isel Park. Keep to the open land with the woodland along the summit ridge on the left and Park

Wood to the right: Mannex and Whellan's Directory for 1847 describes Isel Hall as "surrounded with gently rising eminences finely clothed with wood" which pleasantly enhanced the view.

Keep straight ahead where the path is funnelled between the wood and a wall and continue to a tall stile. Beyond this bear gradually to the right to find the next stile over the crossing fence. Across the middle of the next field look for a tall, lone ash tree which marks the beginning of an ancient track lined with old hawthorns. Cross the beck which runs down from Willie White's Well.

The round fell ahead is Binsey, a northern outpost of the Lakeland fells.

From the beck a stile and gate can be seen in the corner ahead under another old and hollow ash tree. Cross the track to a stile in the hedge and then continue over several more stiles as the ancient hollow of the path goes through old strip fields to a gated lane.

As the track approaches the hamlet of Sunderland fork right and then turn right onto the road for about a mile, crossing the Blumer Beck and passing by Linskeldfield Farm with its sizable tarn. At the T-junction cross the stile straight ahead keeping the woodland fence on the left. Cross the footbridge over the beck and follow the path ahead to a gate and stile where the path changes to the other side of the fence to the next stile where it blossoms into a track.

A bridleway crosses the path above Iselgate Farm but carry on over a stile to follow a hedge to a footbridge and another stile. Down Kirk Hill the path is now accompanied by a line of old oaks and ash trees until it descends to the road almost opposite Isel Church and the start of the walk.

Hedgehog (Sarah Mattocks)

Isel and the River Derwent

Base Point:	Armathwaite Hall entrance - 1¹/₂m/2.5km west of Bassenthwaite village
Map:	Pathfinder NY 03/13
Grid Reference:	NY 209325
Distance:	7³/₄m/12.25km

This walk follows an ancient bridleway close to the River Derwent as far as Isel Church and returns by country lanes with extensive views, ending with a short stretch through fields and woodland.

The route begins near the gateway of the Armathwaite Hall Hotel, a late Victorian mansion standing in extensive grounds and with a fine view over Bassenthwaite Lake. The bridleway, known as Buckholme Lonning, goes along the high walls of the hotel grounds passing Coalbeck Farm on the right and in about a mile comes close to Buckholme Island in the River Derwent and Isel Old Park Wood. Beyond this the river veers away from the track which continues through pleasant fields to Long Close Farm.

After passing through the farm go straight on down the road and in less than a mile come to Isel Bridge with the Church nearby. There is access to the river either by the bridge or behind the Church,

Isel Church (William Reading)

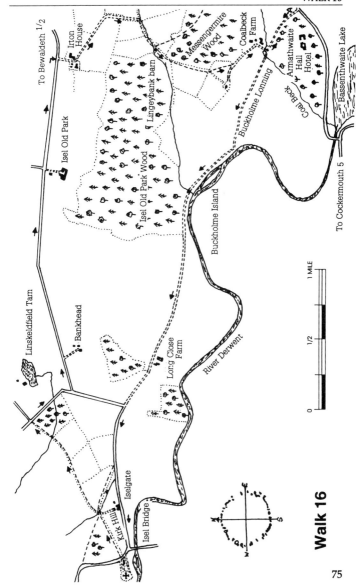

Walk 16

To Bewaldeth 1/2

Irton House

Isel Old Park

Linskeldfield Tarn

Bankhead

Isel Old Park Wood

Lingeybank barn

Messengermire Wood

Coalbeck Farm

Buckholme Lonning

Coal Beck

Armathwaite Hall Hotel

Bassenthwaite Lake

Buckholme Island

River Derwent

Long Close Farm

To Cockermouth 5

Iselgate

Kirk Hill

Isel Bridge

0   1/2   1 MILE

Isel Church interior (William Reading)

a good vantage point to admire Isel Hall across the valley.

The Church of St Michael and All Angels is of early twelfth-century date and much of the Norman structure remains, notably the chancel arch and several windows and doorways. There is much of interest here, not least the delightful churchyard which is particularly attractive in the spring.

To continue the walk turn left along the road outside the church gate for about 100 metres to a path on the right leading to Kirk Hill. This follows a line of old oak and ash trees to a stile and footbridge. Shortly after this cross over a bridleway and carry straight on for a good ¹/₂ mile through several stiles and a footbridge over another beck to join the road by High Calfshaw Wood. Turn right here and in just over ¹/₂ mile turn left along a high road with excellent views of the Derwent valley and the Lakeland Fells. Linskeldfield Tarn is on the left.

A brisk, bracing walk of 1³/₄m (3km) past Isel Old Park Farm brings us to Irton House on the right where a bridleway leads to Bassenthwaite. Enter the farmyard along the drive and bear left in front of the house along a well marked track. It is important to follow the signs, even if the path appears to take a somewhat circuitous route, as this will avoid an area of marshy ground. At the old barn at Lingey Bank the bridleway turns sharply to the left and goes through Messengermire Wood back to the road a few hundred yards east of the Armathwaite Hotel.

Alternatively, it is possible to take the path straight on at Lingey Bank through a wood, along the edge of Messengermire Wood and on to Coalbeck Farm. Turn left along Buckholme Lonning to the starting point.

Walk 17:
Cockermouth and the River Cocker

Base Point:	Main Street, Cockermouth.
Map:	Outdoor Leisure - Lakes NW
Grid Reference:	NY 123307
Distance:	5m/8km

Leave the main street of Cockermouth in a southerly direction up either Station Street or Gallow Barrow which join together to become the Lamplugh Road at the old railway crossing. Lamplugh Road crosses the busy A66 trunk road in a staggered fashion so take great care in crossing and carry on in the direction of Egremont for about 300 metres beyond the A66, where a bridlepath goes left past Waterloo Cottage.

The bridlepath is wide and straight and rises gradually giving good views back over Cockermouth and the Derwent valley and increasingly interesting views of the fells around the Lorton valley ahead. The land undulates enough to obscure the immediate path ahead but from Waterloo, the farm on the left, the bridlepath goes down to a sharp right turn, where our route keeps straight on through a gate, across the Paddle Beck via a footbridge and on

Southwaite Bridge, River Cocker (William Reading)

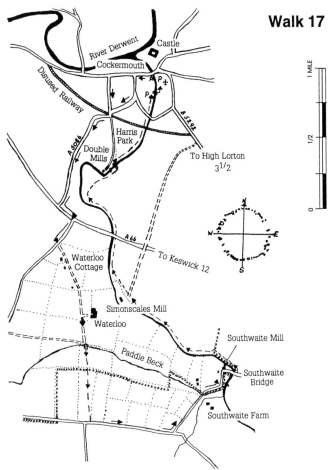

Walk 17

across the field to a gate. From this middle gate the roadside stile can be seen straight ahead and here we turn left down a quiet road, past windswept beech trees, for nearly ¹/₂ mile to the next corner where we turn left again, down to the river crossing at Southwaite.

The River Cocker flows along a wide straight stretch called The Rake before it slides over the weir at Southwaite Mill whose

River Cocker at Southwaite, (William Reading)

buildings occupy the corner by the old bridge. Once over the bridge turn immediately left into the riverside field and look back for a lovely picture of the water glinting in the sunshine, as it falls over the weir, all framed by the arched bridge.

From Southwaite Bridge the riverside path downstream is obvious and well walked by fishermen. It initially scrambles through some riverside bushes and a little further on goes right, up the bank, to avoid a steep corner, but in general it follows the riverside. At the only habitation, Simonscales Mill, the path keeps to the right of the house, crosses the drive by two stiles and continues on towards the river again.

Simonscales Mill is recorded as a paper mill in 1772 and later became a bobbin mill manufacturing bobbins, reels and spindles for the Lancashire and Yorkshire textile industry.

This is a lovely stretch of river with flowers and birds to enjoy and so isolated from the busy world that it comes as a shock suddenly to see the traffic on the A66 hurtling across the valley on a high bridge.

Under the bridge the path keeps slightly right, cutting off a wide sweep of the river and the first building to come into view on the far bank is the youth hostel at Double Mills. The path leaves the field here by a stile and then crosses the river by a footbridge.

Double Mills probably received its name from its two wheels operating in separate channels. The Badgkin Mill on the opposite bank of the Cocker is referred to in 1478 as "opposite the corn mill" indicating that Double Mills is older than this date. It worked as a corn mill for over 400 years: its two French Burr stones may be seen by the mill buildings. Badgkin Mill operated as a fulling mill, a leather mill, a saw mill and as an iron forge making farm tools.

A detour to look at the mill whose old stones can be seen in the yard is worthwhile. Carry on down river by turning right through a gate into Harris Park just beyond the footbridge.

This is a pleasant riverside walk with tall trees, and daffodils in the spring, obviously enjoyed by local people. Where the path rises up a slope round a riverside house, a kissing gate takes the path riverwards or you can carry on along the wide path to join the riverside track beyond the house.

There are now only a few hundred metres along a rather dark damp gorge with the railway bridge overhead before the first chance to emerge into the town at Jubilee Bridge where you turn left towards the town centre. An alternative is to carry on along the river, cross the footbridge and emerge in the car park behind the market place.

Cockermouth

Less than a mile to the north-west of Cockermouth lie the remains of the Roman fort of Derventio, or Papcastle as it is known today. There is little to be seen of it now as most of the stone was carted off to build the castle and other buildings in Cockermouth but excavations have suggested that the fort and its vicus or civilian settlement were once as important and as large as the much more famous establishment at Housesteads on Hadrian's Wall.

Cockermouth first appears in the records in 1150 when the Normans moved their power base from Papcastle to their new castle on a well-defended neck of land at the confluence of the Rivers Derwent and Cocker. Less than a century later, 1221, the new "town" received a charter to hold a weekly market: it had thus acquired the two essentials for urban success - a centre of power and a centre of commerce. Before the thirteenth century had ended the up-and-coming town had been granted various coveted

Cockermouth Castle (Joseph Farington)

rights including the right to send two members to Parliament but this was a privilege it seemed to take very lightly, as no MPs were sent between 1300 and 1640! The establishment of the famous Hiring Fair in 1349 and the rebuilding of the castle by the Earls of Northumberland in the late fourteenth century set the seal on Cockermouth's medieval prosperity. It was now in a strong position to exploit the general economic development of the Tudor and Stuart centuries and to eliminate rival markets at Ireby and Crosthwaite. In the reign of Elizabeth I Camden's Britannia described Cockermouth as "a mercate town of good wealth" with a weekly fair now as well as its Monday market; a century later it claimed to be "ye best Market Towne in this part of ye country.....adorned with a stately Castle, a Fair Church, two good stone bridges, a fair house and many other fine buildings", and according to the Herald's Visitation at this time the town could boast five families worthy to bear arms as against only two in Carlisle and one each in Kendal and Penrith.

Industrial growth in the eighteenth and nineteenth centuries added to Cockermouth's opportunities. The ample waters of the Derwent and Cocker provided power for many mills. The ancient corn and fulling mills were now joined by others manufacturing woollen textiles, hats, gloves, breeches, high leather boots, paper, bobbins and tweed, and by bark mills, sawmills and mills for dressing flax.

Pre-eminent among Cockermouth's industries was Jenning's Brewery, famous long after the mills had had their day, and the provider of ale to the innumerable hostelries which appeared in the town in these years. A few were coaching inns of high repute - the Globe, the Sun, the Appletree, the

81

George and Dragon - servicing the many local and Stage Coaches which passed through each day.

Most of Cockermouth's architectural heritage dates from these prosperous times and the best may be seen in the Market Place, Castlegate and St Helen's Street. The Elizabethan Old Hall suffered many years of neglect and in 1973 was finally condemned and demolished. Cockermouth's most famous house is the birthplace of William Wordsworth, a fine mid-eighteenth-century residence, described in Pevsner's Buildings of England as "quite a swagger house for such a town". This was saved from demolition in the 1930s and is now assured for the future in the hands of the National Trust.

Wordsworth was not the only famous citizen of Cockermouth. Among a long and impressive list perhaps the best known are: John Dalton, distinguished scientist and first to formulate the atomic theory; Fearon Fallows, Astronomer Royal; John Walker, Director of the National Vaccine Board, a keen disciple of Jenner; Abraham Fletcher, mathematician, pioneer of standards of measurement; Richard Southwell Bourke, Sixth Earl of Mayo, Chief Secretary for Ireland and Viceroy of India, MP for Cockermouth; and, of controversial fame, Fletcher Christian, leader of the mutiny on the "Bounty".

Cockermouth is not within the National Park boundary, and this may well have its advantages, but like Kendal, Penrith and Ulverston (also excluded) it has in recent years done much to protect and restore its historic buildings and to improve its attractiveness as an old market town.

Walk 18:
Low Fell

Base Point:	Thackthwaite or Scale Hill car park - in Lorton Vale
Map:	Outdoor Leisure - Lakes NW
Grid References:	NY 148236 or NY 149215
Distances:	5m/8km from Thackthwaite - 6m/9.7km from Scale Hill

Two base points are given for this walk as there is only very limited parking space near Brook Farm, Thackthwaite, and the car park at Scale Hill is only

Walk 18

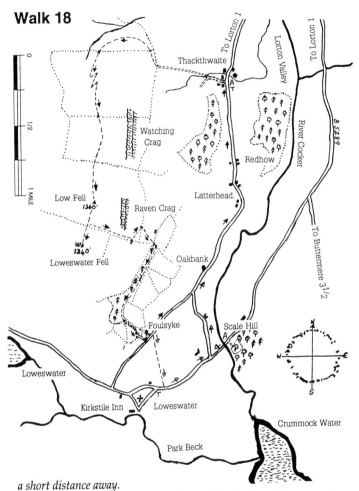

To Lorton 1

Thackthwaite

Lorton Valley

To Lorton 1

B 5289

Watching Crag

Redhow

River Cocker

Low Fell

1360'

Raven Crag

Latterhead

To Buttermere 3½

Loweswater Fell

1340'

Oakbank

Foulsyke

Scale Hill

Loweswater

Kirkstile Inn

Loweswater

Crummock Water

Park Beck

a short distance away.

Note: The path to the summit of Low Fell from Thackthwaite is clear and easy, a gentle stroll, and for much of the way on soft, sheep-cropped turf. The descent to Foulsyke is quite another story, involving a very steep 450 metres drop from the summit with a gradient often steeper than 1:3,

Loweswater (William Reading)

painless and undemanding for the lithe and lissom but a challenging course for those whose joints are not quite as supple as they were. The latter may find it more enjoyable to return to Thackthwaite by the gentler slopes of the drove road along which the ascent was accomplished. This 'there and back' expedition misses none of the views if both summits are visited and is a modest four miles in length.

Route from Thackthwaite:

From the signpost to Low Fell by the roadside at Thackthwaite pass through the farm to join a clear track straight ahead. In 150 metres take the right fork following the slate footpath arrow. The path continues straight ahead over several stiles with a line of old oak trees and a tiny beck for company. On reaching the open fell turn right along a broad, grassy drove road which curves round gently to the left before rising by a series of zig-zags to an easy, straightforward stroll to the summit, the only checks to progress being several simple stiles.

The view from the first cairn is truly grand, embracing an imposing vista of mountain scenery with Crummock Water nestling in the foreground between the great bulk of Grasmoor and the precipitous flanks of Mellbreak. But to appreciate fully the real grandeur of this place you should visit the southern summit of Low Fell, only a short distance further on. Here the scene is completed by the inclusion of Loweswater and the woods, farms and green pastures which surround it. Beyond the immediate circle of fells round Buttermere is an array of Lakeland peaks as magnificent as one is likely to see, a view wonderfully described by Wainwright as one "of classical beauty, an inspired and inspiring vision of loveliness that has escaped the publicity of picture postcards and the poets' sonnets, a scene of lakes and mountains arranged to perfection". This is without question a walk to save for a fine, clear day.

Those who plan to return direct to Thackthwaite will be tempted to linger on this delightful summit; those who wish to pursue the round walk have further to go and, initially, a more arduous route to follow.

From the stile between the two summits go steeply down the fellside with the fence on your right. Keep close to the fence all the way. Not far from the end of the steep section a stile is set in the fence: do not cross over this but turn left to follow the path over to another stile about 200 metres away on the right. Over this stile follow a groove along a line of old thorn trees down, diagonally to the right, to a stile in the fence at the edge of a narrow conifer plantation.

The path through the trees here is almost obscured but the persistence of walkers has kept the right of way open and a well-trodden route will be found going straight ahead from the stile to the end of the plantation where another stile leads into open woodland and a good clear track. This is now a pleasant walk, notable for a fine display of primroses in the spring. At the gate by the buildings at Foulsyke follow the drive through to the road.

Turn left here and continue along the lane for about 1¹⁄₂ miles back to the starting point in Thackthwaite. This is an attractive and quiet lane through part of the Lorton Valley, thoroughly unspoilt by modern development, passing by several old farmsteads surrounded by pastures and woodlands and with extensive

Skylark (Thomas Bewick)

views over the River Cocker to the craggy buttresses of Whiteside and to the forests of Whinlatter.

Route from Scale Hill:
From the car park turn left along the road towards Loweswater and cross the bridge over the River Cocker. In about 250 metres turn right along a road which in under ¹/₂ mile comes to a T-junction. Turn right here and follow the lane for just over a mile to Thackthwaite where a signpost on the left points the way to Low Fell. From this point follow the directions given above as far as the road at Foulsyke. Turn left here for a few yards only to a footpath on the right which goes across the field to the Loweswater Road. Turn left to return to the Scale Hill car park in ¹/₂ mile.

*   *   *

Refreshments on this walk may be obtained at the Kirkstile Inn only a few minutes from Foulsyke.

Walk 19:
Crummock Water, Scale Force and Mosedale

Base point:	Scale Hill car park
Map:	Outdoor Leisure - Lakes NW
Grid Reference:	NY 149215
Distance:	7¹/₄m/11.7km

This is a varied and interesting walk, first through pleasant woodland and then along the western shore of Crummock Water to visit Lakeland's tallest waterfall at Scale Force, returning along a fine bridleway under the crags of Mellbreak and above the valley of Mosedale. There are many fine viewpoints of the lake and of the Buttermere fells, one of the best being that from Lanthwaite Hill, famous as one of Thomas West's "stations" and much in favour in Victorian times but less well-known today. (This may be omitted from the walk if desired, thus reducing the total distance by just under a mile and avoiding a modest climb, but this would miss out one of

Walk 19

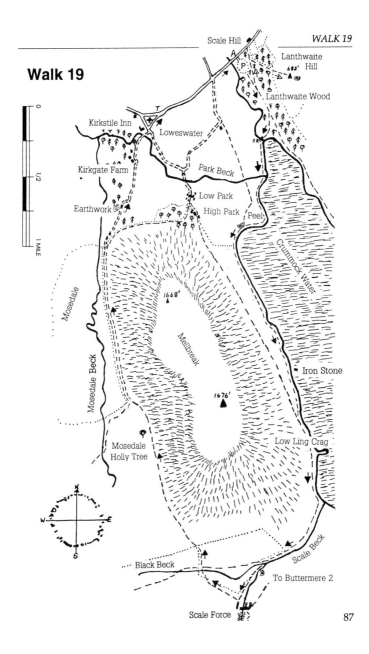

Scale Hill

Lanthwaite Hill

Lanthwaite Wood

Kirkstile Inn

Loweswater

Kirkgate Farm

Park Beck

Earthwork

Low Park

High Park

Peel

Crummock Water

Mosedale

1668'

Mellbreak

Mosedale Beck

Iron Stone

1676'

Low Ling Crag

Mosedale
Holly Tree

Scale Beck

Black Beck

To Buttermere 2

Scale Force

*Scale Force
(William Reading)*

the most impressive scenes in the whole of Lakeland, and it is well to remember that the Victorians were far more sophisticated in their tourism than we are today.)

The walk begins in the Scale Hill car park by following the broad path into Lanthwaite Wood and taking the left fork after a very short distance in order to join a higher path. Turn left along this path for a few hundred metres and look for a narrow path on the right which goes up Lanthwaite Hill alongside a wall. This climbs steadily through the woods and via some zig-zag steps eventually comes to a stile which gives access to the open fell. Follow the winding path to the summit, a delightful little plateau of turf and rocky outcrops, and enjoy a prospect of mountain, lake and wooded valley which has changed little since Thomas West came here 200 years ago.

Descend by the same route to the terrace path above the car park. Turn left along the terrace and continue for about ¹/₂ mile towards the lake shore, taking the right fork at the junctions of paths. When the lake is reached turn right to cross the outlet by the footbridges and so join a path along the western shore.

MOUNTAINS SEEN FROM LANTHWAITE WOOD CRUMMOCK WATER.

1	Whiteless Pike	4 { Great End	5	Scawfell Pike	8 { High Crag
2	Honister Crag	5 { Great Gable	7 { Kirkfell	9 { High Stile
3	Green Gable	{ Rannerdale Knott/beneath)	{ Scarf Gap (below)	10	Blaeberry Crag
			11	Red Pike
			12	Melbreak

Mountains seen from Lanthwaite Wood (Elizabeth Lynn Linton)

Follow the shoreline path round the foot of the lake to join another path which also continues along the western shore.

Near the meeting point of these paths are traces of earthworks marked on the map by the name "Peel". This suggests that at some time there was a fortified pele tower here and there is some slight historical evidence which indicates that this may have been the site of the medieval home of the Lindsay family who, like so many other northern families, built a stronghold for protection against Scottish raiders during the Border Wars.

The walk along the lake continues for a little under 2 miles and may be followed either by the shoreline path or by a broader path at a slightly higher level.

A prominent rock just offshore is known as the Iron Stone, and about half a mile further on is a spit jutting into the lake. This is Low Ling Crag and in former days was the landing-point for the boats which brought tourists across the lake on their way to visit Scale Force.

Almost opposite Low Ling Crag is the rocky eminence of High Ling Crag and just beyond this the path bears right, away from the lake, to follow a well-trodden but fairly rough track by Scale Beck up to a footbridge over Black Beck. Cross this bridge and continue upwards to another bridge almost at the foot of the waterfall.

Joseph Budworth in his Fortnight's Ramble to the Lakes *in 1795 described Scale Force as "a musical abyss" where the water fell some 200*

Pied flycatcher (Peter Gambles)

feet. Wordsworth saw "a lofty chasm with a lofty though slender fall of water". Just how "lofty" this waterfall is appears to be the subject of some dispute: Budworth's 200 feet is reduced to 172 feet by Hunter Davies's Good Guide to the Lakes, *to 160 by Miss Martineau, to 156 by John Murray, to 130 by John Wyatt, to 120 by the* National Park Guide Book *and to no more than 100 by the AA. If Scale Force is, indeed, distinguished as Lakeland's tallest waterfall, it surely deserves to have its height officially and accurately measured!*

To continue the walk find the path which goes fairly steeply up on the *right* of the fall rising diagonally towards a fence on the right. Near the corner of this fence look for a stile which has to be crossed in order to join the route to Mosedale. Once over the stile follow the fence upwards to a second stile. Cross over this and after bearing slightly to the left go straight ahead along a path which follows the contour along the flank of Mellbreak.

The pointed fell across the valley is Hen Comb, perhaps Lakeland's least frequented fell, protected as it is by wide areas of encircling boggy wasteland which are impassable after heavy rain and uncomfortably wet at all times. Mosedale just below our path is one such barrier, a marshy wilderness so devoid of interest that the Ordnance Survey singles out for special mention "The Mosedale Holly Tree", the only tree in Lakeland to be awarded this distinction, a landmark to be noted about three-quarter of a mile along the path from the last stile.

The path joins the main bridleway from Loweswater to Ennerdale ¹/₄ mile further on. Continue straight ahead following what was once a rather grand iron fence. Where the path divides round a small plantation take the left fork down to a gate. Beyond the gate the bridleway passes along a walled lane with fields on either side.

The first field on the left has remains of an ancient earthwork known as Kirkstead. The name suggests that there may have been a chapel or even a pagan structure with religious significance on this site but its origin is unknown.

A brief glimpse of Loweswater enhances the view as the path

passes Kirkgate Farm and soon after this a bridge crosses Park Beck. Adjacent to this is the Kirkstile Inn where excellent refreshments are available and at the nearby road junction is Loweswater Church, mainly Victorian and little more than 100 years old. Pass the church on your left and join the main road at the next junction. Bear right and follow the road for the ¹/₄ mile back to Scale Hill car park.

Walk 20:
Loweswater

Base Point:	Loweswater Church
Map:	Outdoor Leisure - Lakes NW
Grid Reference:	NY 142209
Distance:	7m/11.25km

There is limited car parking space at the road junction near Loweswater Church but this walk may also be started from two other base points where alternative space is available. These points are indicated by an asterisk on the map. The car park at Scale Hill is more spacious and is half a mile away to the north-west.

If an alternative base point is used the walk directions can be readily adapted with the aid of the map.

In 1865 Mrs Lynn Linton, a formidable and perceptive explorer of the Lake Country, visited Loweswater and wrote with enthusiasm of her walk round the lake which she described as "very choice. Only a seven mile walk or so, and yet how many of the thousands visiting our country yearly even dream of taking this walk into their experience". Loweswater is somewhat better known today but compared to Grasmere, Rydal or Buttermere it is still well away from the tourist trail. Yet, as Mrs Linton observed, this walk is one of the most charming and interesting in the whole of the Lake District. We do not follow her precise route which included the long stretch along the road - then a pleasanter place to stroll than it is today - but we do join her on the delightful paths through Holme Wood before taking the superb high-level terrace walk with its view over the lake and into the truly impressive array of mighty fells above Crummock Water and Buttermere with their ever-changing colour and their slopes of intimidating steepness.

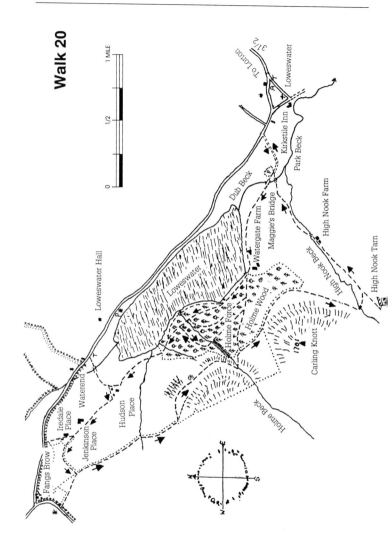

Walk 20

Crummock Water from Loweswater Church (William Reading)

Loweswater Church is a nineteenth-century replacement of an earlier chapel and is a good example of solid Victorian craftsmanship but with no claims to architectural originality. The earliest chapel on this spot was founded in the early twelfth century by Ranulph de Lindsay who presented it, with a parcel of land, to the Priory of St Bees.

From the church take the road past the Kirkstile Inn and turn left at the junction soon passing by the school which was built in 1839 to accommodate eighty children! 200 metres further on turn left at the signpost indicating a public bridleway, a narrow, hedged and metalled lane with an abundance of spring flowers and a fine close-up view of Mellbreak, with Crummock Water to the left and Loweswater on the right.

Just beyond the bend at the end of the lane is a National Trust sign and a small car park. Two bridges cross over Dub Beck here: an old stone bridge known as Maggie's Bridge on the left and a distinctly functional structure on the right which is the one to choose at this stage in the walk to join the broad track across the meadows to Watergate Farm.

Dub Beck is the outflow from Loweswater and its direction makes this lake unique in Lakeland. All other lakes flow outwards away from the fells; Loweswater flows inwards and via Dub Beck and Park Beck its waters find their way into Crummock Water.

The track to Watergate approaches the lake just before reaching the farm and just beyond the farm enters Holme Wood.

Watergate Farm, High Nook Farm, Holme Wood and the lake itself are all properties of the National Trust. The two farms date from the early eighteenth century and are among the prized possessions of the Trust as they acquired a wealth of very fine woodwork during the Regency Period, the money for which may have come from the profits of local lead mines. The lake has been restocked with brown trout and the nesting sites of many water birds are protected from disturbance. The wood is now managed to a very high standard and pleasanter and more delightful mixed woodland would be difficult to find. Towering pine trees and other fine conifers accompany a great variety of native broadleaves and the forest floor is a tapestry of celandines, wood anemone, wood sorrel, violets, bluebells and other wild flowers while the chorus among the treetops makes it clear that this is a safe and welcome haven for many species of birds.

As the map shows there are several clear paths through Holme Wood and any may be chosen to walk along to the far end. The route described here keeps close to the lake and makes a short diversion to visit Holme Force.

Follow the main track beyond the gate into the wood along the lake side. A variety of birds may be seen on the water and, perhaps, a hopeful angler. In a few hundred metres the Holme Wood Bothy is reached. This is an ancient barn now converted into simple accommodation for voluntary workers who help the National Trust

in the summer season. Just beyond this the path divides: the right-hand path follows closely to the shoreline while the main ride continues straight ahead, either may be followed.

To make the short detour to Holme Force take

Jay (Sarah Mattocks)

the second main track on the left beyond the bothy by a group of tall pine trees. (If you have followed the shoreline path you should turn back along the main ride for about 200 metres when you rejoin it and then, of course, turn right by the pines.) Climb steadily up through the wood and after the path bears to the left the waterfall will be clearly heard and will soon be seen. This diversion should take only a few minutes to accomplish.

Holme Force is a succession of spouting cascades and pools falling precipitously through a high larch plantation. Whitewater sprays glisten in the sunlight as they arc above green pools spilling over to slide darkly over slipways and to atomise yet again over the next downfall. In a final flourish the water divides into two spouting jets which splash and disperse among a pile of boulders on the very edge of the path.

From the waterfall return to the main path by the same route.

Turn left and continue to the gate at the end of the wood. Beyond the wood the path goes straight ahead and alongside a recently rebuilt stretch of dry stone wall - a tribute to the waller's craft. A stile and gate lead into a narrow lane which leads to Hudson's Place, the first of three ancient farmsteads on the next stage of the walk.

At the head of the lake here is Waterend, the scene in July 1865 of a memorable few days by Loweswater spent by a party of forty-four Quakers from Manchester who were the guests there of Rachel and Robert Jackson. Food, accommodation and a change of clothing were provided for this large gathering who attended the Quaker Meeting at Pardshaw, picnicked by the lake, climbed Carling Knott and thoroughly enjoyed themselves before setting off for the return journey at 4 o'clock in the morning.

The lane bears right in front of the house at Hudson's Place. It is easy to miss the sign in a short distance which indicates the next stage of the walk. Immediately past a cottage named "The Place" look for a gate on the left marked with a blue arrow. No path is visible in the field beyond this gate but this is, in fact, a bridleway and a succession of blue arrows will confirm this. Follow the hedge to a stile where an arrow points the way to the right along another hedge to another stile and another arrow.

Continue straight ahead up a short bank which can, at times, be very wet and muddy, and on to a gap in a wall as one approaches Jenkinson's Place. Bear slightly to the left across the field to a gate which leads into a real bridleway passing close by the farm. The lane

Red squirrel
(Thomas Bewick)

is metalled for a short distance before it forks. The bridleway and our route proceed along the left fork as indicated by the blue arrows at Iredale Place.

The name "Place" attached with the owner's name to a farmstead was in the eighteenth century something of a status symbol, intended to indicate that the farmstead was primarily a "residence" rather than a farm. All the "places" just passed were built in the eighteenth century, incorporating parts of older structures.

Continue up to a gate and here turn left to follow a wall to a ladder stile where a signpost indicates the various routes. Take the left turn signposted "Loweswater via High Nook".

The broad track ahead follows the wall closely for $2/3$ mile (1km) to a gate and stile where a blue arrow points firmly to the left - but take the lower track beyond the gate; the upper track leads nowhere.

The next stage of the walk is one of the finest terrace walks in the Lake District, a comfortable stroll along a grassy, well-made, high-level walkway, with a birdseye view of Holme Wood and a grandstand view of the group of peaks beyond Crummock Water with Mellbreak in the foreground. Loweswater itself is, as Thomas West saw it 200 years ago, "spread out before you, a mile in length and about a quarter of a mile in breadth. The extremities are rivals in beauty of hanging woods, little groves and waving enclosures, with farms seated in the sweetest points of view." To encourage fuller appreciation of this uplifting scene a wooden seat, simply carved with walking boots and oak leaves, has been placed on a well-chosen site along the way.

The track swings to cross Holme Beck $1/4$ mile beyond the seat and then follows closely to the boundary wall of Holme Wood. A gate marks the beginning of the long gently-graded descent to High Nook, first passing under the crags below Carling Knott and then crossing the footbridge over High Nook Beck, a fast-flowing stream

St Bega's church, Bassenthwaite
Ennerdale

which has its source in the marshes high on Gavel Fell. It receives a small tribute from a nameless tarn, hidden in a shallow depression just above the footbridge - nameless, that is, until Wainwright appropriately dubbed it "High Nook Tarn".

Continue the descent to High Nook, a fine Lakeland farmstead in a charming setting of burbling becks, green pastures and shady trees, and with the beck beside you complete the journey back to Maggie's Bridge and to the starting point of the walk.

Walk 21:
Flat Fell and Nannycatch Gate

Base Point:	Kinniside Stone Circle - 1½m/2.5km south of Ennerdale Bridge
Map:	Outdoor Leisure - Lakes NW
Grid Reference:	NY 061141
Distance:	3m/4.8km (5m/8km if the summit of Dent is included)

This is a pleasant little walk in a remote and almost unknown corner of the National Park. Nannycatch is a delightful miniature ravine hidden among the plantations of Uldale Forest and beneath the slopes of Flat Fell, a modest eminence distinguished only by its precipitous screes which fall steeply down to Nannycatch Beck. The walk starts from the stone circle at Kinniside where there is space to park several cars, but there is also an official Forestry Commission car park just off the road about ½ mile further on.

The circle of standing stones at Kinniside, officially known as Blakeley Raise Circle, is one of the seventeen neolithic or early Bronze Age megalithic circles still surviving in Cumbria. They belong to the same mysterious culture as Stonehenge, Avebury and other similar structures but their origin and purpose remain unexplained. That they were related to some ritual or ceremony seems almost certain but whether these occasions were of a religious nature we can only speculate upon. Many of the circles, like

Wastwater Screes

Walk 21

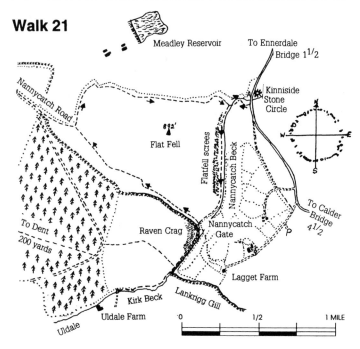

that at Kinniside, have burial cairns within them, and this may have some significance, but the precise alignment of the stones has led to a theory that they were constructed on remarkably complex mathematical calculations based on the movements of the sun and the moon. Professor Thom has calculated the unit of measurement as a megalithic yard or 2.72 feet and on this basis the diameter of the perfect circle at Kinniside is exactly 20 megalithic yards. Furthermore, he claims, a line from the tallest stone through the centre of the circle to Screel Hill marks the setting point of the moon at its maximum cyclical northerly setting. Whatever their skills in astronomical mathematics may have been, we can at least admire our Bronze Age ancestors' choice of site with its magnificent views of the Cumbrian coast, the Irish Sea, the Isle of Man and the hills of Dumfries and Galloway. It is a pity that an enterprising but misguided amateur archaeologist took it upon himself earlier this century to dig up these stones *and set them in concrete without leaving any record of his "reconstruction"! This has led some to believe that the whole circle is bogus but experts now accept it as genuine.*

The walk starts across the road, almost opposite the stone circle, where a path descends fairly steeply to Nannycatch Beck. Cross the beck and follow the path to the left alongside it. This soon becomes a good track passing under Flat Fell Screes and in about ²/₃ mile arrives at Nannycatch Gate, a charming and secluded glade, a sheltered watersmeet, a perfect trysting-place for outlaws, conspirators and romantic lovers.

(From this point it is possible to extend the walk over the boundary of the National Park to climb to the summit of Dent which at 1131 feet commands a spectacular view of almost the entire coast of Cumbria from the Solway Firth to Black Combe and an unexpected and unfamiliar prospect of the Lakeland fells which includes Skiddaw, Grasmoor, Pillar and the Scafells. The route to Dent is indicated on the map but there is no public footpath. The distance

Kinniside Circle (Robert Gambles)

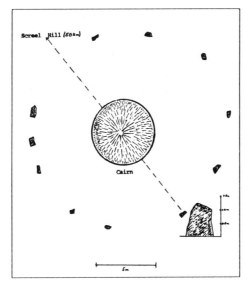

from Nannycatch Gate to the summit is about 1 mile. On the return descent care must be taken to follow the same route down to Kirk Beck in order to avoid the hazards of Raven Crag.)

The 3-mile walk continues from Nannycatch Gate by following the bridleway between Raven Crag and Flat Fell. The forest fence on the left marks the western boundary of the Lake District National Park. In a little under a mile the path comes to the corner of a drystone wall. Here the bridleway goes off to the left along Nannycatch Road but our route turns right, close to the wall and gently up the fellside. (An easy ascent of Flat Fell is possible from this point but the view is disappointing and is really not worth the effort.)

Within the space of one mile the path alongside the wall transports one from a prospect of the fringes of industrial Cumbria with an overview of the town of Frizington and the many quarries nearby, through pleasant pastoral scenery surrounding Meadley Reservoir, to a sudden, startling and majestic vista of the towering fells beyond Ennerdale.

Follow the wall all the way until it descends to Nannycatch Beck. Cross the beck and climb up to the road to the stone circle where the walk began.

Cuckoo (Thomas Bewick)

Tongue Moor and the River Calder

Base Point:	Cold Fell Gate - 4m/6.5km south of Ennerdale Bridge
Map:	Outdoor Leisure - Lakes SW
Grid Reference:	NY 056101
Distance:	8³/₄m/14km

This is the longest walk in the book. It is in lonely and remote country. Good footwear and sufficient supplies of food and drink for several hours are essential. It should not be attempted in thick mist as the paths on the open moors, ancient bridleways though they may be, are occasionally not clear on the ground. Worm Gill has to be forded and this could present problems after prolonged or heavy rain.

Even so, this is an exhilarating route with varied scenery and excellent views. It passes by the oldest packhorse bridge in Cumbria and several old farms whose names remind us of the Norse settlements and of the proximity

Monk's Bridge, High Wath (William Reading)

Walk 22

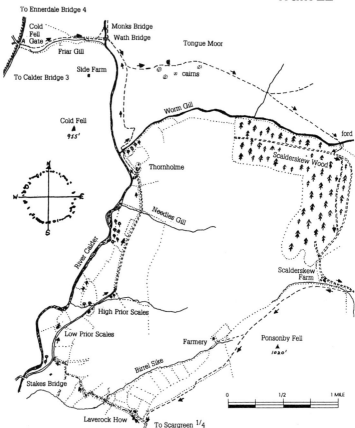

of Calder Abbey. The lanes and hedgerows are rich in wild flowers and the cairns and hut circles of a Bronze Age settlement are, as always, mysterious and enigmatic. It is a walk full of interest and challenge. Choose a bright and clear day.

The starting point is at Cold Fell Gate on the Fell Road 4 miles south of Ennerdale Bridge. There is convenient parking space for several cars. Take the broad track opposite the road coming in from Haile and Egremont and follow this down alongside Friar Gill to the footbridge over the River Calder at High Wath.

A very short distance upstream from here will be found, hidden in a tiny ravine, a lovely true packhorse bridge, probably the oldest now remaining in Cumbria, and known variously as Monk's Bridge, Matty Benn's Bridge and Hannah Benn's Bridge. It is very narrow with a pointed arch and has no parapets (to allow the easy passage of wide panniers) and it is thought to be the bridge once used by the monks of Calder Abbey to give access to their iron bloomery at Thornholme nearby. It is well worth a visit.

Return to the wooden footbridge and continue along the track going up the fellside above the river. Some 300 metres up this track look for a very narrow path on the left leading on to Tongue Moor directly opposite Side Farm high above the far bank of the river. The path soon fades in the moorland grass but it never disappears

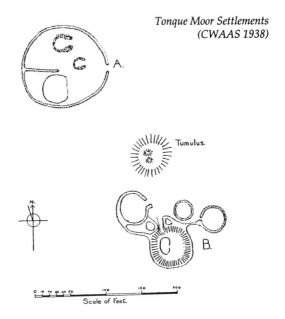

Tonque Moor Settlements
(CWAAS 1938)

A.

Tumulus.

N.

B.

Scale of Feet.

103

entirely. Keep Side Farm always in line behind you and soon, on the brow of the rising moor, the stones of the ancient settlement will appear. The path goes right by the largest hut circle and close to the most prominent cairn.

It is not possible to put a precise date to this settlement but it is probably Bronze Age. The existence of so many remains on these moors and the evidence of terraced cultivation enclosures on the southern slopes would seem to indicate a once permanent and flourishing community, enjoying a settled life and a fine view to the westward sea.

Continue straight ahead to the east and very shortly pass by another large cairn on the right of the path. From here descend very slightly to the right and the path soon becomes a good, clear track. On the far bank of Worm Gill below is Scalderskew Wood and at its distant eastern edge is the ford which is the next objective.

The path descending to the ford is not, at first, easy to follow but it soon becomes quite clear. Note the boundary of the forest plantation opposite; just beyond this and immediately before the broad track swings away up to the moors on the left a tiny beck crosses the path. At this point a rather indistinct path goes diagonally down in a direct line towards the ford. It may disappear from time to time in the wet patches but after a while it develops into a clear and well-defined route ending at the ford itself.

If the water is low the ford may be easily crossed on the stones or, if preferred, it is not difficult to wade across.

*IF THE WATER IS HIGH TAKE NO RISKS: CALL OFF THE
EXCURSION.
THERE IS NO ALTERNATIVE ROUTE.*

After negotiating the ford go through a gate up on the right and into the forest. Follow the path steeply upwards for a short distance to the main forest road. Turn left for a few metres and then take a track on the right which is the right of way. Proceed along here in a straight line for approximately $1/2$ mile where the forest road is rejoined. Bear right here and soon come to a cattle grid on the left leading on to the road past Scalderskew Farm which is reached in a few minutes after leaving the forest.

Scalderskew is a remote and lonely spot approached by road only through Blengdale Forest. It is first recorded in the thirteenth century as Scalderscogh or Skjoldr's Wood.

Continue along the road past the farm for a few hundred metres to a bridleway sign pointing the way to Scar Green. This doubles back on the way you have come and goes through a gate into the field behind the farm.

At first there is no visible bridleway or path of any kind but follow a line fairly close to the farm fence on the right and, just above the farm, a good track suddenly appears leading off across the moor in a westerly direction.

You are now on the flanks of Ponsonby Fell, a dull, uninteresting eminence of just over 1000 feet, damned for all time by Wainwright's pronouncement that it is very nearly not worth climbing, being tedious to ascend, possessed of a dreary summit and enjoying only a limited view.

About ½ mile from Scalderskew the bridleway divides. The right fork goes across towards a group of farm buildings and a banked enclosure known as "Farmery", a name derived from "Infirmary", for on this site stood the "convalescent home" of Calder Abbey. Our route takes the left fork and soon comes to a gate in a wall. Through the gate follow the path along the fence and continue in the same direction with the fence eventually on the right. The rough fields here are the spring nesting grounds of many curlews which wheel and cry above the heads of the few humans who pass this way.

Curlew (Sarah Mattocks)

Follow the fence all the way down to a sunken lane. Turn right here to the old farm of Laverock How.

A few of the buildings here are of some antiquity and include a "Scandinavian" or "bank" type barn found only in the areas of Norse settlement in Lakeland and the Yorkshire Dales.

Go through the farm to a gate and into a walled and hedged lane which continues down to cross over Birrel Sike. Bear slightly left here and, through a gate, follow the lane round a number of abrupt turns and through several gates to join the metalled road.

Turn right along the road, a quiet lane running almost parallel to the Calder, go past the farms at Low Prior Scales and High Prior Scales and so to a gate which gives access to the road leading to Thornholme Farm.

Just before Thornholme is reached turn left off the road along a bridleway (signposted) down to the junction of the River Calder and Worm Gill, a pleasant place to rest and prepare for the final mile or so back to base.

Cross the footbridge and look up on the right for a good track on the flank of the round, tumulus-like, mound in front. After a brief climb this track takes a sharp turn to the left to rise steadily to the level moor above the Calder. In a little over $1/2$ mile this will return you to the footbridge over the river at High Wath and so back to Cold Fell Gate.

Walk 23:
Nether Wasdale

Base Point:	Nether Wasdale Church
Map:	Outdoor Leisure - Lakes SW
Grid Reference:	NY 125041
Distance:	5m/8km

This is an easy and delightful walk through the gentle and varied landscape of Nether Wasdale, a fascinating pattern of mixed woodlands and ancient hedges, grassy hummocks and rocky knolls, water meadows and marshy hollows. Old Lakeland farmsteads and fine Victorian residences are set among rhododendron groves and magnificent oaks and beeches; the fresh green of sheep pastures vies with the manicured turf of carefully tended lawns. And all are watered by many tiny becks flowing into the River Irt, England's finest salmon river, which, in turn, flows from Wastwater, at 258 feet England's deepest lake. On this walk, too, is the most famous viewpoint in the Lake District, the classic view over the lake of Wastwater's precipitous screes with Great Gable beyond in its superb mountain setting.

Walk 23

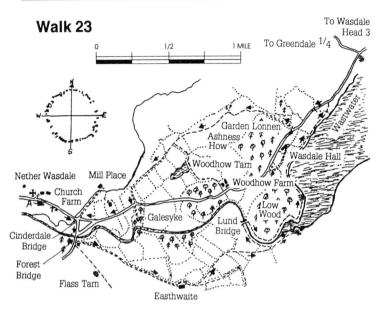

The walk begins at the Church of St Michael and All Angels, Nether Wasdale, a typical dales church but with some interesting seventeenth-century carved panels from York Minster.

Follow the road eastwards out of the village passing Church Stile Farm on the left and in a short distance come to the bridge over the Cinderdale Beck. Turn right here and cross the River Irt at Forest Bridge. Just beyond the bridge turn left along a track signposted to "Lake Foot". This leads to Easthwaite Farm where the path goes between the buildings with the farmhouse on the right.

At a gate beyond the farm take the path bearing to the left across the fields (the path straight ahead leads to Hawl Gill) and pass through several gates. When a path veers off to the left towards Lund Bridge continue straight on towards the lake as this offers the best view of the screes. From the lake foot return along the path by the river bank and walk to the crossing at Lund Bridge: the low-lying meadows here are a favourite haunt of many butterflies.

Cross the river and immediately beyond the bridge turn right

Wastwater and Great Gable (Margaret Woods)

into Low Wood, an interesting mixture of deciduous trees and conifers with a colourful carpet of flowers in the spring and early summer. Follow the bridleway through the wood down to the shore of the lake where a good lakeside path provides an opportunity to enjoy the spectacular view of Lingfell, Yewbarrow and Great Gable seen over (and often reflected in) the dark waters of Wastwater.

Continue along the shore soon passing below Wasdale Hall, a modest mansion with mock Tudor half timbering and mullioned windows, built substantially in the nineteenth century and now a youth hostel. The path passes through a grove of rhododendrons and soon afterwards emerges on to the road. Turn left along the road, cross a cattle grid and in about 200 metres turn right into a wide lane with High Birkhow Wood on the left-hand side of it. This lane is known as Garden Lonnen, a name derived from an Old English word for a lane and from the walled enclosure on the right which used to be the kitchen garden of Wasdale Hall in its heyday. At the end of the lane is a ladder stile which has a grandstand view of Buckbarrow Crag.

Bear to the left over the stile and follow the path as it meanders among the rocky hummocks towards Ashness How. Aim for a footpath sign at a junction and from here follow the path ahead signed to Galesyke. This eventually becomes a walled lane with a centuries-old dyke on the left which now supports a remarkable

Great tit
(Thomas Bewick)

variety of trees and shrubs.

Country lore has it that by counting the number of different shrub species along a 100 yard length of hedge it is possible to calculate the age of the hedge in centuries. On this basis the hedge here must be at least 600 years old, as approximately six species may be found in any one length, a number which is doubled for the whole hedge, a rare feature.

At the end of the lane rejoin the metalled road almost opposite the entrance to Galesyke. Turn right along the road and in about $^1/_2$ mile return to the church.

Walk 24:
Muncaster Fell

Base Point:	Eskdale Green Station
Map:	Outdoor Leisure - Lakes SW
Grid Reference:	SD 145997
Distance:	6$^1/_2$m/10.5km

As the Rivers Mite and Esk run their parallel courses towards the sea at Ravenglass they are separated for the last few miles by a long, isolated fell of modest height, with an impressive northern flank and a gentle summit ridge, which has magnificent views out to the sea and into the mountains. This is Muncaster Fell. Heather and bilberry and the bronze of the autumn bracken colour its wide, open spaces, and rhododendrons, gorse and extensive woodlands adorn its slopes. Under the northern crags runs the famous Eskdale miniature railway while under the southern flank is the line of the Roman road from Ravenglass to Ambleside. At the seaward end

Walk 24

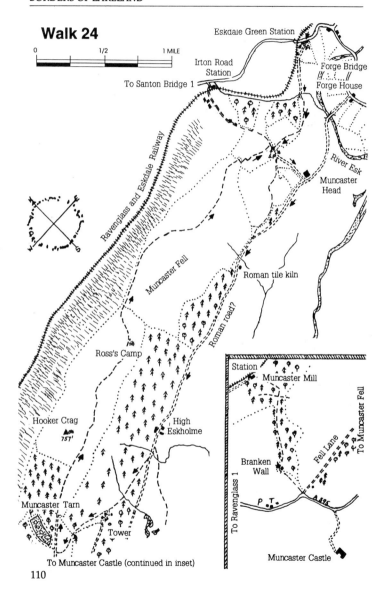

0   1/2   1 MILE

Eskdale Green Station

Irton Road Station

To Santon Bridge 1

Forge Bridge

Forge House

River Esk

Muncaster Head

Ravenglass and Eskdale Railway

Muncaster Fell

Roman tile kiln

Roman road?

Ross's Camp

Hooker Crag
757'

High Eskholme

Muncaster Tarn

Tower

To Muncaster Castle (continued in inset)

Station

Muncaster Mill

Fell Lane

To Muncaster Fell

Branken Wall

To Ravenglass 1

P T

A595

Muncaster Castle

stands Muncaster Castle, home of the Penningtons since the thirteenth century, and Muncaster Mill, medieval in origin and now restored to a working water-mill with its eighteenth-century machinery still in operation. On the fell itself Ross's Camp at an easily attained height of 700 feet offers a truly enchanting panorama of Eskdale, Miterdale and the Lakeland fells.

Note: The full circuit of the fell described here may be too strenuous and time-consuming for those who also wish to visit the castle and the mill. An attractive alternative is to leave the car near Muncaster Mill and to take the train from the station there to Eskdale Green, described by some as "the most beautiful train journey in England". From here the fell ridge may be traversed as indicated and the castle reached along the Fell Lane in less than four miles. A pleasant walk of about one mile completes the route back to Muncaster Mill (see inset map).

The castle is open daily, except Mondays (bank holidays excepted), from April to the end of October, 1pm to 4pm; the gardens are open daily from 11am to 5pm. Muncaster Mill is open to visitors from April to October, 11am to 5pm. The train service operates approximately every hour, more frequently in July and August.

There is only limited parking available at Eskdale Green but alternative space may be found ½ mile south in a wide lay-by near Forge Bridge over the River Esk.

Good footwear is advisable for this walk. For the most part the path is excellent but there are a few places which, after a spell of wet weather, can be soft and muddy.

A signpost by the roadside near Eskdale Green Station points the way to Muncaster Fell. Join this bridleway which runs past the station and, for a short distance, keeps company with the railway. It then continues along a walled lane down to a beck. Cross the beck by simple stepping stones and follow an indistinct path across the field always keeping fairly close to the wall on the right. At the end of the wall, swing to the right by a grove of oak trees and cross the next field to a gate, a stile and a collection of signposts. Turn left here taking the track to Muncaster Head Farm which is reached in a few hundred metres.

Turn right at the farm along a good, hard-surfaced track which may have been the line of the Roman road. Follow this for just over 1½ miles to High Eskholme with extensive plantations on one hand

111

Henry VI Tower,
The Chapels,
Muncaster Fell
(William Reading)

and the wide green pastures of the Esk water-meadows on the other.

Near the Parkhouse plantation a Roman tile kiln was discovered and excavation revealed it to have been of some importance. An official notice advises you of its presence but only a grassy mound is outwardly visible.

Just beyond the buildings at High Eskholme a bridleway goes off to the left: do not follow this but look for a blue arrow bridleway sign a few metres further along the road on the right. This leads to a grassy lane up the fellside. Follow this up through the wood to a group of cottages.

Nearby is a tall, stone tower, octagonal in plan and three storeys high, with lancets, cross-slits and circular openings in the walls. This is known as the Tower of Chapels, and the domed ground floor with its large niches, seems to suggest that this may well have been its original purpose. It was erected about 200 years ago to commemorate the supposed discovery by local shepherds on this spot of King Henry VI after his flight from defeat at the Battle of Towton in 1461 during the Wars of the Roses. This story owes more to romantic legend than to proven historical fact but it is perpetuated in the tale of the "Luck of Muncaster", an enamelled glass drinking bowl, said to have been presented to the Pennington family at Muncaster Castle where the King found refuge. The bowl is still with the

Swinside stone circle
Dunnerdale

The Lickle valley
Beacon Tarn

Penningtons and attached to its history is the legend that as long as it remains intact the family will have good fortune and continue to live at Muncaster.

Continue through the wood to a small gate which leads into an open, park-like area with graceful groups of silver birch and massive rhododendron bushes. The path swings round to the right to join the broad track leading to Muncaster Castle and the summit of Muncaster Fell. Turn right for the open fell which is reached through a gate in just under 1/4 mile. Before this you may wish to take a look at Muncaster Tarn hidden away a few metres from the bridleway on the left. It may be reached by a path through the bushes.

From the fell gate the path goes straight ahead traversing the entire ridge of the fell. The main path keeps to the Eskdale side and for the best views this is the route to follow but the energetic may like to make a diversion to the summit of Hooker Crag, the highest point at 758 feet.

Half a mile beyond Hooker Crag the path passes by Ross's Camp, a massive rock slab resting on assorted boulders, vaguely reminiscent of some Neolithic tomb but in fact erected in 1883 as an amusing diversion by a shooting party: an excellent seat to rest awhile, a fine table to spread your picnic, and with a marvellous view over Eskdale and to the sea.

Muncaster Castle (Muncaster Estate)

Continue to follow the well-trodden path to a gate by the corner of drystone walls and then descend across a rather wet depression which is succeeded by a short climb among scrub. Proceed downhill for a little under a mile alongside a wall of Eskdale granite to a stile in a cross wall. Soon after this the path bears to the right and arrives back at the complex junction of routes with a varied assortment of stiles, gates, gaps and signposts. Look for the sign pointing to "The Green and Station" and follow the path across the field, round the wall, down to and over the beck and along the lane to the station where the walk began.

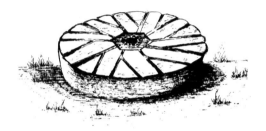

Millstone with master and slave furrows (Sylvia Rigby)

Walk 25:
Stanley Ghyll

Base Point:	Trough House Bridge, Dalegarth, Eskdale
Map:	Outdoor Leisure - Lakes SW
Grid Reference:	NY 173003
Distance:	1¹⁄2m/2.3km

Convenient parking for cars near the start of this walk is available either close by Trough House Bridge or (for patrons of the miniature railway) at Dalegarth terminus. A pleasant day's outing could be planned by taking the Eskdale Railway from Ravenglass (where cars may be parked) to

Walk 25

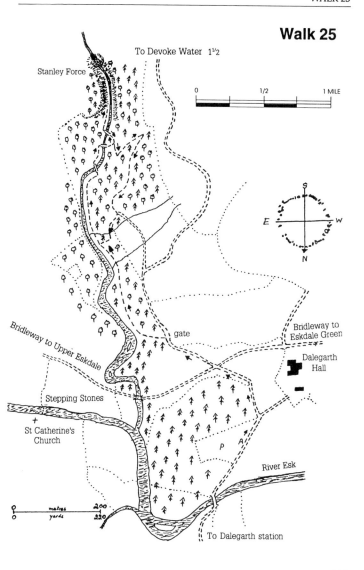

To Devoke Water 1¹/2

Stanley Force

0   1/2   1 MILE

Bridleway to Upper Eskdale

gate

Bridleway to
Eskdale Green

Dalegarth
Hall

Stepping Stones

+
St Catherine's
Church

River Esk

P A

metres   200.
yards   220

To Dalegarth station

Stanley Ghyll Force (William Reading)

Dalegarth Station. This walk starts less than quarter of a mile from the station. There is a frequent train service in the summer months.

    Stanley Ghyll Beck gathers its waters from the bleak uplands of Birker Fell and after pouring over one of Lakeland's most spectacular waterfalls continues through an airy woodland garden to meet the River Esk near the stepping stones to St Catherine's Church. This is an easy and charming walk full of interest all the way. The well-made path clings to the beckside through the ravine with plenty of pleasant spots to pause to admire the scene or to study the many varieties of plants, flowers and trees along the way. Of special interest are the mosses and ferns which grow abundantly here forming cushions of brilliant green among the rocks and trees. Stately

116

St Catherine's Church, Eskdale (H.William Reading)

conifers mix comfortably with more familiar deciduous trees, and from the early spring until June rhododendrons blaze a trail of colour to the very lip of the fall. The waterfall, known as Stanley Force or Dalegarth Force, drops cleanly some 20 metres into a deep pool enclosed by precipitous rocks, an enchanted spot.

The path from Trough House Bridge passes Dalegarth Hall with its five round Cumbrian chimneys and from 1345 the home of the

Stanleys who gave their name to Stanley Ghyll. Just beyond the Hall the track crosses the bridleway from Upper Eskdale to Eskdale Green and shortly afterwards a gate in the wall on the left bears a sign "To the Waterfall".

Grey Wagtail (Thomas Bewick)

117

Through this gate a broad path leads directly to the beck and then continues clearly all the way to the falls, passing over the beck three times by good footbridges. The fall is just above the third bridge and care is needed beyond this point.

DO NOT ATTEMPT TO CLIMB BY THE FALL: IT IS HIGHLY DANGEROUS

The return walk may be made by the same route but may also be varied by a short diversion from a point above the middle bridge where an alternative path is clearly marked.

Walk 26:
Devoke Water and Barnscar

Base Point:	Near to summit of the fell road from Ulpha to Eskdale
Map:	Outdoor Leisure - Lakes SW
Grid Reference:	SD 172977
Distance:	3m/4.8km or 5^1/2m/8.8km

Sections of this walk are marshy and may be at times very wet. Good footwear is essential. The walk starts at the signpost near the summit of the fell road from Ulpha in the Duddon Valley to Eskdale. There is a convenient parking space here for several cars.

Take the rough track to the west immediately opposite the road coming from Stanley Ghyll and signposted to Waberthwaite.

Devoke Water soon comes into view and is reached in a little over ^{1}/2 mile. On the left near the shore is the rocky eminence known as Seat How towering abruptly to more than 1000 feet and occupying a dominating position overlooking the lake.

The boathouse marks the end of the track. Take the path along the lake-shore, a route not always easy to follow in the frequent marshy patches. It is difficult to believe that this was once a major bridleway to Waberthwaite and thence to Ravenglass.

Along the shore line here you may see a few anglers fishing for brown trout but secretly hoping to catch one of the golden variety introduced to

Walk 26

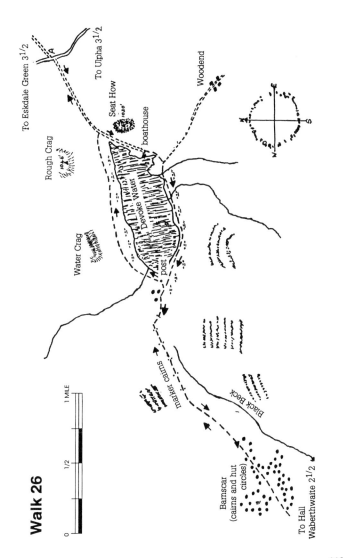

To Eskdale Green 3¹/₂

To Upha 3¹/₂

Rough Crag

Seat How
1020'

boathouse

Woodend

Water Crag

Devoke Water

post

marker cairns

Black Beck

Barnscar
(cairns and hut
circles)

To Hall
Waberthwaite 2¹/₂

0   ¹/₂   1 MILE

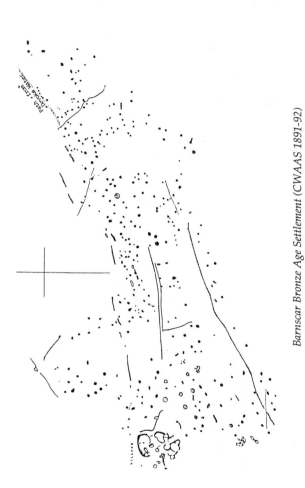

Barnscar Bronze Age Settlement (CWAAS 1891-92)

these waters by the monks of Furness Abbey some 400 years ago - and still happily breeding here.

On reaching the far end of the lake aim for a prominent wooden post by an ancient cairn above the shore on higher, drier ground. From here one can begin the extended walk to Barnscar or complete the circuit of Devoke Water.

The walk to Barnscar is over undemanding terrain and is quite exhilarating, utterly remote from the modern world, the silence broken only by the cry of curlews and peewits, the cronk of a colony of ravens and the song of the many skylarks which nest among the tussocks.

For Barnscar follow the grassy path westwards. This is marked at intervals for some distance by pairs of stones. This "avenue" comes to an end near a sheepfold but is succeeded by a line of large and prominent cairns. The first ruined hut circles of the Bronze Age settlement soon begin to appear and straight ahead will be seen the slight eminence on which the main settlement was established.

Here, over 400 cairns, enclosures and hut circles, 15-25 feet in diameter, are an impressive reminder, even in their ruinous state today, that some 3000 years ago this was a well-populated village, supported by the fertile and well-stocked woodlands which clothed these bleak moorlands and by the cereals grown in the small fields cultivated nearby. For many centuries it was known locally as 'the city of Barnscar'. The site commands a wide vista over the sea and a breathtaking view of Great Gable and the high fells around it.

Return to Devoke Water by the same path.

To continue the circuit of the lake descend from the wooden post towards the other shore and cross Linbeck Gill by a small waterfall. The area near the lake is wet and it is best to make for the higher ground where a reasonably good route can be found. There is no regular path, but the sheep,

Raven (Thomas Bewick)

121

which have a sound instinct in these matters, have established several well-used trods avoiding most of the wettest parts. Keep well above the lake among the grass and scrub and the result is a pleasant stroll back to the main track near the boathouse.

Walk 27:
Swinside Stone Circle

Base Point:	Broadgate - off A595, 2m/3.25km SW of Duddon Bridge
Map:	Pathfinder SD 08/18
Grid Reference:	SD 182867
Distance:	6m/9.7km

Black Combe stands detached and isolated in the south-west corner of the National Park. It is a massive eminence covering many square miles of moorland and marsh, rocky outcrops and precipitous crags, deep combes and grassy plateaux. Bracken, bilberry and heather grow in colourful abundance on the higher slopes; wild flowers and bright green mosses flourish by the becks which flow from this mighty gathering ground. This is lonely country now but, as numerous ancient cairns and the megalithic circle at Swinside testify, it was well-known to our neolithic ancestors.

The main route to the summit is a wide, grassy bridleway described by Wainwright in his Outlying Fells. *The walk outlined here does not go to the summit but lies on the eastern edge of the mountain and visits the stone circle at Swinside with an exploration of the little-known territory between Black Combe and the Duddon Valley.*

The walk begins near the hamlet of Broadgate $^1/_4$ mile off the A595 between Broughton-in-Furness and Millom. A section of the old road - signposted "Broadgate" - provides a number of safe and suitable parking spaces.

Join the Fell Road to Broadgate and follow this for about $^1/_2$ mile where, just before Crag Hall, a stony lane goes off on the left with a footpath sign to Swinside Stone Circle and Thwaites Fell. From here it is approximately 1 mile to Swinside Farm. The circle of stones stands in a level field just before the farm buildings. On the way a

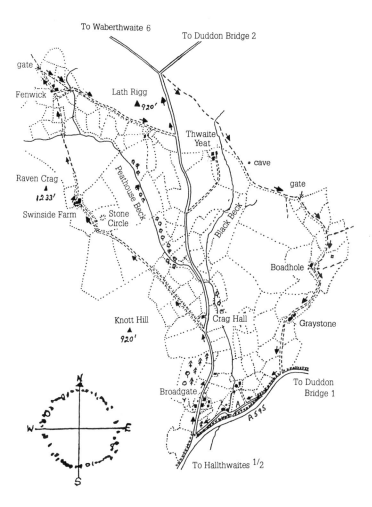

0   1/2   1 MILE

Walk 27

To Waberthwaite 6

To Duddon Bridge 2

gate

Fenwick

Lath Rigg

▲ *920'*

Thwaite Yeat

○ cave

gate

Raven Crag

▲ *1233'*

Swinside Farm

Peathouse Beck

Stone Circle

Black Beck

Boadhole

Knott Hill

▲ *920'*

Crag Hall

Graystone

Broadgate

To Duddon Bridge 1

A595

To Hallthwaites ¹/2

N

W   E

S

wide prospect of the Duddon Estuary unfolds to the south while all around is pastoral country and in the distance the jagged peaks of the Dunnerdale fells are outlined against the sky like miniature Alps. Pass through a gate into a field and in a few paces another gate gives access to the stone circle.

Of the 250 or so stone circles in England 65 are known to have been in Cumbria and of these Swinside, Castlerigg near Keswick, and Long Meg near Penrith, are among the oldest. This means that this almost perfect circle of megaliths - of which 51 still remain - was erected here, perhaps some 4000 years ago, for a purpose still largely unknown to us. It seems very probable that these great monuments were the "temples" of some religious cult and were used for sacred and ceremonial occasions with, no doubt, elaborate rituals and processions. At Swinside excavations have shed no light on the mystery and nothing of significance has been found, but, as with all other megalithic circles, this, too, appears to have been constructed with considerable skill and mathematical precision. Whether the design of these circles and the placement of the stones was specifically related to the seasonal solstices and to the movements of the sun and the moon is a fascinating but still unproven theory. The entrance at Swinside is at the south-east where two large and additional stones outside the circle act as imposing portals.

The local - and the Ordnance Survey - name for the monument is "Sunkenkirk" or the sunken church, a description arising from a belief that the Devil caused the stones of a church here to subside into the ground. Swinside stands in a magnificent setting, an appropriate place for us to ponder awhile on the achievements of our predecessors here so many centuries ago. A diagrammatic representation of the Swinside Circle forms the compass points on the maps of the walks in this book.

To continue the walk go forward to the farm buildings, pass round them to the left and just beyond the house go through a gate leading to a track over an open area of field and marsh. When the track peters out continue straight ahead in a direct line across a damp patch of ground and down to a footbridge over the beck. This is a pleasant spot and for those who wish to combine a visit to the circle with a fairly short walk this is a good place to turn back along the same path to Broadgate, making a round trip of under 4 miles.

If you wish to press ahead cross over the footbridge and aim up the slope to the white mark on the fence. Cross into the next field, go

Swinside Circle (Margaret Woods)

straight ahead to the next white-painted stile, cross this and go forward to another white stile.

(The white paint splashed lavishly on every stile here is an intimation that for the next half a mile you must keep very strictly to the legal right of way.)

Proceed directly towards the farm at Fenwick. Keep straight on between the farm buildings following the track to the left of the farmhouse until you come to the well-head of a spring at the side of the track a little further on. Here it is tempting to make a bee-line for the (white-painted) stile over on the right which is, in fact, the next objective but in order to keep to the right of way you should continue along the track to a gate just beyond the well. From here the right of way now cuts back sharply across the field and down to the stile quite close to the farmhouse. Cross this stile and proceed directly to the next one. After this join the track leading away from the farm. Cross the beck and through the gate enter a pleasant lane which leads in a good ¹/₂ mile to the fell road.

Turn left along the road with a truly splendid view before you of the fells beyond the Duddon to the distant blue of the highest peaks. In ¹/₄ mile is a T-junction with a signpost pointing to Millom, Broughton and Whitehaven. Here the path goes off at a sharp angle to the right in a direct line with the road coming from Whitehaven. Look for a grassy groove across the open moor and follow this in a fairly straight line, passing Thwaite Yeat farm near the corner of a well-built wall. The path keeps close to the wall passing by an old quarry cave under the crags of Barrow. About ¹/₂ mile from Thwaite Yeat the second gate in the wall indicates the way to Boadhole.

Go through this gate and follow the path by a broken wall, passing through a gate with a blue bridleway arrow, and eventually coming to a wall at right-angles to the path just before Boadhole. The precise line of the right of way here is still undetermined: legally it passes over the stile in the wall but, as will be obvious, an easier alternative made by other walkers is clearly visible through the gate on the right. This leads to the house at Boadhole.

From Boadhole go through the gate opposite the house and into the lane which goes past Graystone House down to the main A595 trunk road. Turn right along the road, walk along the verge for a few hundred metres to rejoin the minor road to Broadgate where the walk began.

Herdwick sheep (Herdwick Society)

Ulpha Park and Frith Hall

Base Point:	Ulpha Bridge: Duddon Valley, 3m/4.8km north of Broughton-in-Furness
Map:	Outdoor Leisure - Lakes SW
Grid Reference:	NY 906931
Distance:	5m/8km

In the early fourteenth century Lady Alicia de Huddleston established an extensive deer park at Ulpha and late in the following century one of her descendants built a hunting lodge there, known today as Frith Hall. This walk passes through part of the ancient park, now planted with mixed woodland, visits the ruins of the lodge and rambles pleasantly along the banks of the River Duddon. It is an easy walk full of interest and starts at Ulpha Bridge where there is usually parking space for several cars.

Cross the bridge to the western side and turn left at the road junction along the fell road to Bootle. Follow this road for a little over ¹/₂ mile to Bobbin Mill Bridge over Holehouse Gill, with the Duddon not far away to the left and Rainsbarrow Wood below The Pike to the right.

The buildings of the old bobbin mill have been converted into private houses but the remains of the great chimney still stand by the roadside, a strong stone pillar to remind us that this was once a busy industrial site where men and boys worked long hours in deafening noise and swirling dust, slaves to endlessly repetitive work at fast-moving and dangerous machinery. This was one of the fifty or so Lakeland bobbin mills which in the mid-nineteenth century supplied more than half the requirements of the country's textile industries, a total of several million bobbins each week. The nearby River Duddon provided a cheap and abundant supply of food for the apprentices at the mill: so abundant, indeed, that, clearly suffering from a surfeit, they negotiated a clause in their contract which stipulated that they were not to be given salmon more often than three days a week.

Opposite the mill and immediately over the bridge is a public footpath sign. Follow this through a gate and along a track beside the gill. This is the start of the old pack-horse trail to Millom and,

Walk 28

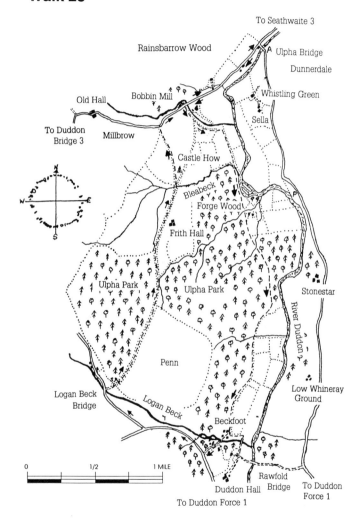

To Seathwaite 3

Ulpha Bridge

Rainsbarrow Wood

Dunnerdale

Whistling Green

Bobbin Mill

Old Hall

Sella

To Duddon
Bridge 3   Millbrow

Castle How

Bleabeck

Forge Wood

Frith Hall

Stonestar

Ulpha Park

Ulpha Park

River Duddon

Penn

Low Whineray
Ground

Logan Beck
Bridge

Logan Beck

Beckfoot

0   1/2   1 MILE

Rawfold
Bridge

Duddon Hall

To Duddon
Force 1

To Duddon Force 1

Frith Hall (Margaret Woods)

over Corney Hill, to the west coast. This very soon bears right but our path goes straight on by the gill and in about 400 metres swings to the right alongside a field wall to a gate giving access to Forge Wood. Through the gate cross over Blea Beck and continue along a good track with the Duddon watermeadows on the left and pleasant mixed woodlands on the right.

The name "Forge Wood" and the evidence of coppicing among the trees is a reminder of the old woodland industries which once flourished here. These woods supplied the Duddon iron furnaces with charcoal and the bobbin mills with thousands of poles of all sizes, and must have been alive with sounds of woodcutters, bark-strippers, charcoal burners and many others involved in the woodland industries which made the Furness woods so vital a part of the early industrial revolution. The Duddon Bridge Iron Furnace is situated approximately one mile south of the limit of this walk. It is one of Cumbria's most important historical monuments and is well worth a visit. It operated as a blast furnace from 1736 to 1867 and is now the most complete surviving charcoal fired blast furnace in England. Its recent restoration won a prestigious heritage award.

In about $1^{1}/_{2}$ miles the path arrives at Beckfoot, a delightful little woodland settlement whose buildings once housed a fulling or "walking" mill where coarse, loosely woven textiles were matted,

Duddon Furnace (Margaret Woods)

felted and shrunk by men walking on rolls of cloth immersed in troughs of water and fuller's earth, a process later performed by trip hammers.

As you cross the bridge over the Logan Beck note the original narrow structure shown by the remaining stonework in the road surface and by the alteration visible on the underside of the arch. Go straight on between the houses and join a narrow tarmac road which in a few hundred yards comes to the fell road between Duddon Bridge and Bootle. Turn right here and walk up the hill to a road junction. Take the right turn and in a little over ¹/₄ mile cross the bridge over Logan Beck. This is a peaceful spot to rest by the water's edge after the hard roadwork from Beckfoot.

Just beyond the bridge look for a track on the right through the woods of Ulpha Park, now mainly pine and spruce whose tangy scent is mingled with the fragrant aroma of the bog-myrtle growing in profusion along the woodland rides. At the end of the forest pass through a kissing gate and across a rough pasture with a marsh on the left, a nesting site for snipe and curlew. The ruins of Frith Hall will be seen over a slight grassy knoll on the right.

It is possible to reach the Hall by going through a gate or gap in the fence by the field wall, and while the gaunt, ivy-covered fingers of the ruined walls may at first arouse no more than passing curiosity, their setting is a glory to behold. High above the Duddon Valley with its river, woods and pastures, Frith Hall offers a vista which extends far beyond the cottages of Ulpha and the Dunnerdale Fells to the distant, dark-blue ramparts of the highest Lakeland Fells. One turns back to the pathetic ruins perhaps more curious to know something of the story of an ancient building occupying such an exceptional site.

As a hunting lodge Frith Hall was owned by the Huddleston family for many generations possibly succeeding Old Hall, a short distance away, which may have been a fourteenth-century pele tower. Their royalist sympathies in the Civil Wars of the seventeenth century cost the Huddlestons dearly and resulted in a severe decline in their fortunes. Frith Hall was abandoned and became an inn, acquiring a somewhat dubious reputation. Its wild and romantic setting and its remote situation on a minor coach road (Daniel Paterson included Frith Hall Road as a coach route in his celebrated Road Book published in numerous editions in the early years of the nineteenth century) made it an ideal refuge for eloping couples, and runaway marriages were performed here on the same lines as those at Gretna Green. In 1730 alone, no less than seventeen such marriages were celebrated in these rooms, now obscured by piles of fallen rubble and open to the sky. Such a place must inevitably have its ghost and you may meet

Dipper (Thomas Bewick)

here the spirit of William Marshall, "sojourner", who was, apparently, murdered at the inn on 10th October 1736.

Return to the track and follow it down to Bleabeck Bridge, formerly a packhorse bridge but later widened. Through the gate beyond the bridge the route goes straight ahead with the prominent rocky hill of Castle How on the right. The path goes directly to a gate by the road at the top of Millbrow.

(The remains of the Old Hall may be seen by turning left along the road at Millbrow and walking up the hill for rather less than $^1/_2$ mile.)

Turn right down the hill, pass the bobbin mill once more, and so return along the road to the bridge at Ulpha.

Walk 29:
The Lickle Valley and Appletreeworth Beck

Base Point:	Hawk Bridge - 1$^1/_2$m/2.5km north-east of Broughton Mills, 4 miles south-west of Torver.
Map:	Outdoor Leisure - Lakes SW
Grid reference:	NY 239919
Distance:	6$^1/_2$m/10.5km or 4m/6.5km

This is an easy walk along country lanes and woodland paths in one of the most unfrequented corners of the Lake District. The starting point at Hawk Bridge over Appletreeworth Beck is reached along narrow roads either from Broughton Mills, north of Broughton-in-Furness, or from Torver, south of Coniston village. The route of the walk has no steep gradients, no difficult stiles and only a few marshy patches. There is much lovely pastoral scenery with splendid views of the Dunnerdale Fells and the Duddon Estuary. The River Lickle and its tributaries, the Black Moss, the Long Mire and the Appletreeworth Becks are never far away from the paths.

From Hawk Bridge walk along the lane in a southerly direction and in about $^1/_4$ mile take the right fork at the crossroads. Continue on the road for another $^1/_2$ mile to a signpost in the hedge on the

Walk 29

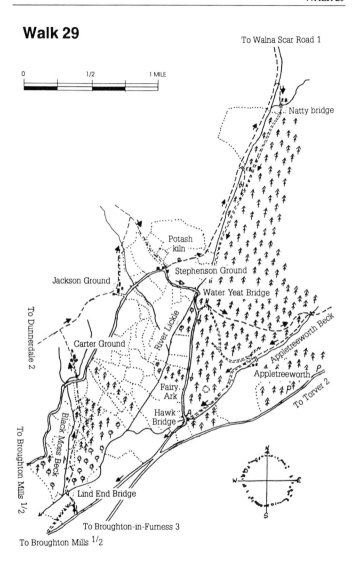

To Walna Scar Road 1

Natty bridge

Potash kiln

Stephenson Ground

Jackson Ground

Water Yeat Bridge

River Lickle

To Dunnerdale 2

Appletreeworth Beck

Carter Ground

Appletreeworth

To Torver 2

Fairy Ark

Hawk Bridge

Black Moss Beck

To Broughton Mills 1/2

Lind End Bridge

To Broughton-in-Furness 3

To Broughton Mills 1/2

*Lind End Bridge
(Margaret Woods)*

right-hand side. This points the way to Carter Ground. Over the stile descend towards the farm buildings and cross a stile between them. Pass in front of the farm-house at Lind End, through a gate across the driveway and then go down the field to the right and under the trees to Lind End Bridge. This is a tiny bridge over the River Lickle, without parapets and hidden away in a wooded gorge, a place of secrecy and charm.

Follow the path up into the woods, passing close to a charcoal burner's platform or pitstead just above the bridge. A gate at the end of the wood leads to an open area and to another gate into a field with plantations on either side. Go through a gap in the wall ahead and soon after passing a group of Lawson Cypress trees go through another gap which has an old gate post or stoop bearing the name "Carter" and the date 1663. Cross the field to a gate leading into a dense conifer plantation. The path beyond this gate is wide and clear and eventually emerges from the trees to cross two stiles and a field before reaching the road by a ladder stile.

Cross the road to enter the driveway to Carter Ground with Black Moss Beck purling on the right. Over the cattle grid walk by the buildings at Carter Ground passing through the colourful garden to a gate leading on to the open fell. A few hundred metres up the fellside, at the junction with the broad track coming from Dunnerdale, turn right towards Jackson Ground.

Jackson Ground is one of the many "grounds" to be found in the Furness area. These were farmsteads carved out from the lands of Furness Abbey and usually bear the name of the first tenant. There are 36 such grounds in Furness, most of them established by an agreement with the

Abbot of Furness in the early years of the sixteenth century. Three are passed in the course of this walk and others in the vicinity include Hartley Ground, Pickthall Ground, Stainton Ground, Hobkin Ground, Greaves Ground and Whineray Ground.

From Jackson Ground continue up the fellside with the wall on the right and just beyond its end cross over Long Mire Beck. Shortly after this at the junction of paths turn right and pass through a gate to join a walled track leading to Stephenson Ground. Here, a signpost on the left indicates the way to Walna Scar.

* * *

For those who prefer to follow the shorter walk the route continues along the road from Stephenson Ground down to Water Yeat Bridge. This is a pleasant and picturesque spot where the banks of the Lickle are adorned with spring primroses and the bushes are alive with small birds. Over the bridge the road passes through mixed woodland, lovely at any time of the year and frequented by deer and red squirrels. A small enclosure has the quaint name of "Fairy Ark". The car park at Hawk Bridge is reached in just over 1/2 mile from the bridge at Water Yeat.

* * *

To continue the longer route from Stephenson Ground, follow the sign-posted bridleway towards Walna Scar, a good, grassy track easy to walk and with fine views of the jagged skyline of the Dunnerdale Fells.

The Lickle Valley
(Margaret Woods)

135

Red stag (Peter Gambles)

A few metres along the track is an old potash kiln close by the path. These kilns were used to produce the potash needed to make soft soap or lye for the fulling or scouring process in the many woollen mills of southern Lakeland, in this case probably the mill at Broughton Mills a few miles away down the Lickle Valley. The stone cistern contained a copper cauldron which was filled with bracken or birch twigs: a fire in the tunnel underneath roasted the contents of the cauldron to leave a potash residue to which lime and water were added. The resulting caustic potash was boiled with tallow to produce the lye. This kiln was probably last used about 100 years ago.

The bridleway continues high above the river all the way to the end of the plantations on the far bank. Just before the end of the trees a bridge made of a stone slab crosses the river; it is possible to shorten the walk by crossing here and following the path into the forest to join the main route within a few hundred yards. Otherwise continue along the bridleway beyond the forest where a narrow ravine will be seen on the right-hand side. Keep straight ahead for a short distance until it is possible to cross the beck onto dry ground just above the marshy area. From here turn back towards the ravine and to the wooden footbridge which crosses it - known as Natty Bridge - noting the plants and bushes which cling precariously to the rocks in the cleft.

Enter the forest and follow a gentle descent along a broad forest path with occasional glimpses of the river through the trees which are an interesting mixture of Norway Spruce, Lawson Cypress, Sitka Spruce and Larch. In about 1 mile take the left fork at the junction of paths and then join the good bridleway into Appletreeworth Forest. This waymarked route crosses several forest roads before reaching a bridge over Appletreeworth Beck and passes through first a belt of mixed deciduous trees and then a plantation of conifers.

Do not cross over the bridge but take the path to the right which follows the beck all the way down to Hawk Bridge through a mile of pleasant woodland.

About half-way along this path is the ruined farmstead of Appletreeworth, once a thriving hamlet among lush meadows but now a deserted melancholy scene, hemmed in by dark plantations, but in spring at least, ablaze with primroses, celandines, violets, golden saxifrage, wood anemones and the delicate shimmer of young birch leaves.

Walk 30:
Beacon Tarn and Beacon Fell

Base Point:	Water Yeat - $^1/_2$m/0.8km south of Coniston Water
Map:	Pathfinder SD 28/38 & Outdoor Leisure - Lakes SW
Grid Reference:	SD 288892
Distance:	$4^1/_4$m/7km

This is a well known round walk much acclaimed for the extensive view from Beacon Fell which embraces the Lakeland fells from Black Combe to Helvellyn and High Street, the Pennine ridge and Ingleborough, and the wide sweep of Morecambe Bay. It is also a famed vantage point from which to survey the whole length of Coniston Water. For the naturalist the walk offers the decorative mixed woodlands along the shores of the lake and a selection of heathers, mosses and bog plants on the Blawith Fells with an interesting assortment of wild birds, stoneflies and moths including especially the emperor and the furry northern eggar. The hummocky terrain on Beacon Fell has spawned a multitude of paths offering a wide choice but if the general direction given on the map is followed there should be no real problem.

The base point for the start of the walk is Water Yeat but there are car parks and several parking spaces along the road by the lake between Water Yeat and Brown Howe. Wherever you park you should make your way along the road to Water Yeat, turn west off the main road and in about 100 metres turn into the lane leading to Greenholme Farm, which is reached in under $^1/_2$ mile. Greenholme is an old farm which has been in the same family for several generations and once operated a mill for the manufacture of pill

Walk 30

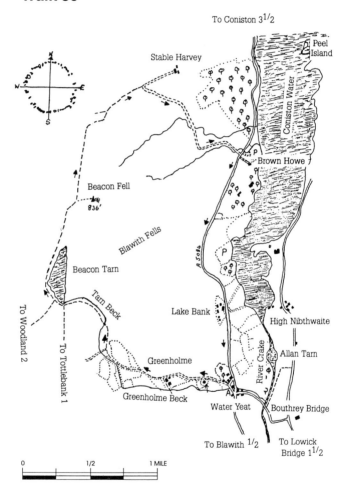

To Coniston 3$^{1}/_{2}$

Peel Island

Stable Harvey

Coniston Water

P

Brown Howe

Beacon Fell
836'

Blawith Fells

Beacon Tarn

Tarn Beck

Lake Bank

P

A 5084

High Nibthwaite

To Woodland 2

To Tottlebank 1

Allan Tarn

Greenholme

River Crake

Greenholme Beck

A

Water Yeat

Bouthrey Bridge

To Blawith $^{1}/_{2}$

To Lowick
Bridge 1$^{1}/_{2}$

0   1/2   1 MILE

Beacon Tarn (William Reading)

boxes.

Continue straight ahead past the farm on a track signposted "To Beacon Tarn" with a wall running along on the left. The track soon becomes a walled lane with Greenholme Beck cascading over the rocks in the wood to the left.

Beyond the wood the track emerges on to the open fell and soon crosses a small footbridge over Tarn Beck. (Ignore a track going off to the left towards Cockenskell.) The path now becomes much narrower but remains quite clear and follows the course of the beck all the way up to the southern tip of Beacon Tarn.

The path continues along the shore of the tarn and joins a major track on the west bank. This is the Cumbria Way, a long-distance footpath running through the Lake District from Ulverston to Carlisle. Follow this along the water's edge to the end of the tarn and then up the ridge to the summit of Beacon Fell.

As the name implies this was once one of the chain of beacons whose fires gave warning of impending raids by the marauding Scots, a not uncommon excitement in medieval times. It is now the spot from which to admire the view referred to above. Those with a liking for historical romance will know that Coniston Water was once known as Thurston Water named after Thorstein, Viking hero of W.G.Collingwood's novel Thorstein of the Mere *who, with his wife, Raineach, made a home and*

Coniston Water from Beacon Fell (William Reading)

refuge from his enemies on Peel Island, "a small island lying all alone in the midst of Thurston Water ....When you see it from the fells it looks like a ship in the midst of the blue ripples ... a ship at anchor .... while tall trees stand for the mast and sails." Peel Island is now protected by the National Trust.

From the summit of Beacon Fell follow the main path steadily down over the heathery hummocks in a north-easterly direction. In a little over ¹/₂ mile pass under the power lines to join a metalled road which links the farm of Stable Harvey with the main road below. Turn right to descend along the tarmac lane through a jungle of oaks, hollies, birches and juniper to join the road just above the car park at Brown Howe. Base point at Water Yeat lies just over a mile along the road to the right towards Blawith.

Blue tit (Thomas Bewick)

Walk 31:
Bigland Barrow and Bigland Tarn

Base Point:	Grassgarth - 2½m/4km south of Backbarrow, near Newby Bridge
Map:	Pathfinder SD 28/38
Grid Reference:	SD 358821
Distance:	4m/6.5km

This is the exception in a collection of "round walks" and must be more accurately described as a "there and back walk". The countryside near Bigland has a network of footpaths and lanes from which it is possible to create a round walk but too much roadwork is best avoided and many of the paths have been so scarred by horses' hooves or by tractors that they are at times no longer pleasant to walk on. The route outlined here includes the best features of the area and as far as possible avoids these hazards. It is a walk of many surprise views - vast seascapes, a beautiful tarn in a lovely setting, a sudden and breathtaking panorama of the highest Lakeland fells - and a stroll through delightful woodland and over soft, springy turf among the limestone outcrops.

The starting point of the walk is at Grassgarth but there is no car parking space nearby and it is, therefore, necessary to add a short walk along the lane to the distance. There are a few spaces near the junction of the lane to Grassgarth and the road from Backbarrow to Field Broughton - approximately ½ mile away.

The first surprise of this walk is its actual starting point which is through a small gate into the garden of Grassgarth House. Pass through the garden to another gate and join a path above Stribers Beck to enter High Stribers Wood. There is a good, clear path through the woods climbing steadily to reveal glimpses of the Leven estuary and the Greenodd Sands. This is delightful woodland, light and airy, and with an interesting variety of trees and flowers.

At the gate at the top of the wood turn left along the wall and follow the grassy path round to the right over Bigland Heights and gently down to the edge of the tarn set in the parkland of Bigland Hall.

Walk 31

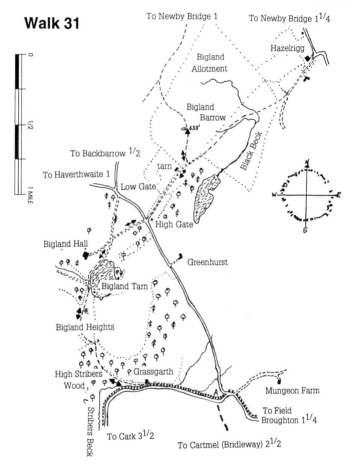

The Hall itself is now an outdoor recreation centre offering facilities for horse-riding, windsurfing, archery, swimming, orienteering and other sports.

A short distance beyond the tarn the path joins the driveway to the Hall. Turn right here and walk to High Gate, the upper entrance to the Park. Cross the road here to a gate and signpost pointing the way to Hazelrigg. Follow the path for about 600 metres to a gate on the left which gives access to Bigland Barrow. A short climb brings one to the modest 630 foot (193 metres) summit which is still adorned by a concrete observation tower dating from the Second World War. More impressive and perhaps totally unexpected is the truly magnificent view of many of the principal Lakeland fells, ranging from Black Combe in the west, through Coniston Old Man and Bowfell to the Langdale Pikes and Fairfield, and, to the north, Red Screes. Wansfell and the distinctive outline of Yoke, Ill Bell, Froswick and the High Street ridge. Away to the east is the long, blue line of the distant Pennines.

Descend from the summit by the same path; that is to say in the direction of the large (and nameless) tarn below. Then return to Grassgarth by the same route followed on the outward walk.

Heron (Thomas Bewick)

EG 24/11/99

Printed by CARNMOR PRINT & DESIGN
95-97 LONDON ROAD, PRESTON, LANCASHIRE, UK.